OLIVIA JONES

MENTAL
EXERCISE
FOR
DOGS

THE 101 BEST DOG GAMES

With Tips And Easy-To-Follow Instructions
To Keep Your Dog Mentally Stimulated, Improve Behavior,
Agility, Intelligence, And Have Fun Together

Dogs bring immense joy, love, and companionship to our lives, and it is our responsibility as dog owners to provide them with the best care possible. Whether you're a new dog owner or have had dogs in your life for years, this book will equip you with valuable knowledge and practical tips to ensure the well-being and happiness of your furry friend.

Chapter by chapter, we will delve into various aspects of dog care and training, covering essential topics that every dog owner should be familiar with. From establishing a strong bond and effective communication to providing proper nutrition, exercise, and mental stimulation, this book will guide you on a journey towards creating a loving and fulfilling relationship with your dog.

In the first section, we will explore the fundamental principles of dog care. We will discuss the importance of understanding your dog's unique needs, including their breed characteristics, temperament, and health considerations. Proper nutrition is also a vital component of their well-being, so we will delve into the world of dog food, addressing topics such as choosing the right diet, portion control, and identifying potential dietary allergies or sensitivities.

Next, we will dive into the fascinating realm of training and behavior. Building a strong foundation through positive reinforcement techniques, we will explore the essential commands your dog should learn for obedience. We will cover training tips, strategies, and common mistakes to avoid, ensuring a successful and enjoyable training experience for both you and your dog.

Beyond obedience, mental stimulation is a key aspect of a dog's overall well-being. Dogs are intelligent creatures who thrive on mental challenges and enrichment activities. We will delve into the realm of mental exercises and games that engage their minds, prevent boredom, and enhance their cognitive abilities.

As social creatures, dogs also require socialization and interaction with both humans and other animals. We will discuss the importance of socialization and provide tips on introducing your dog to new environments, people, and other pets in a safe and positive manner.

Furthermore, we will explore the fun side of dog ownership, discovering various activities and games that you can enjoy with your furry friend. From outdoor adventures and water games to indoor playtime and mental puzzles, we will provide a plethora of ideas to keep both you and your dog entertained and connected.

Whether you're seeking to improve your dog's behavior, enhance their well-being, or simply strengthen your connection, this book is here to guide you every step of the way. Your furry friend is counting on you, and with the knowledge and insights gained from this book, you will be well-equipped to meet their needs and provide a life filled with happiness and fulfillment. Let's dive in and begin this exciting adventure together!

1

Understanding Your Puppy

Grasping the Understanding of Your Puppy

Bringing a new puppy into your life is an exciting and joyful experience. However, along with the fun and cuteness comes a great responsibility to understand and meet your puppy's needs. Building a strong connection with your furry friend is not just about cuddles and playtime—it is crucial for their overall well-being and the development of a harmonious human-canine relationship. Lets's discuss the importance of understanding your puppy and how it benefits both of you.

1. **Enhancing Communication and Relationship**

Effective communication is the foundation of any successful relationship, including the bond between a puppy and their human companion. Understanding your puppy's needs, desires, and emotions enables you to communicate with them more effectively. By learning their unique body language, vocalizations, and cues, you can interpret their messages and respond appropriately. This enhances your ability to provide for their needs, leading to a deeper sense of trust, understanding, and companionship.

2. **Meeting Physical and Emotional Needs**

Puppies, like all living beings, have essential physical and emotional needs that must be met for their well-being. By understanding these needs, you can ensure that your puppy lives a happy and healthy life.

- Physical Needs: Puppies require proper nutrition, exercise, rest, and hygiene. Understanding their dietary requirements and providing a balanced diet promotes their growth and overall health. Regular exercise helps expend their energy, keeps them physically fit, and prevents behavioral issues caused by boredom or excess energy. Sufficient rest and sleep are vital for their growth and development.

Maintaining good hygiene through grooming, regular veterinary care, and cleanliness keeps them comfortable and prevents potential health problems.

- Emotional Needs: Puppies also have emotional needs that should be addressed. They require love, attention, socialization, and mental stimulation. Providing affection, spending quality time together, and engaging in activities they enjoy strengthens the emotional bond between you. Proper socialization exposes them to different environments, people, and animals, fostering their confidence and reducing the likelihood of fear or aggression. Mental stimulation, such as training exercises and interactive play, keeps their minds active and prevents boredom.

Understanding your puppy's physical and emotional needs allows you to create an environment that promotes their well-being, happiness, and balanced development.

3. Facilitating Training and Behavior Management

One of the essential aspects of understanding your puppy is grasping their behavior and learning processes. Puppies are constantly learning and adapting to their surroundings. By understanding their behavior patterns, motivations, and learning styles, you can effectively train them and manage their behaviors.

Training

Understanding how your puppy learns enables you to use appropriate training techniques and methods. Positive reinforcement, which rewards desired behaviors, has proven to be highly effective in training puppies. By understanding their motivations, you can use treats, verbal praise, and play as rewards, making the training process enjoyable and engaging for both of you.

Behavior Management

Understanding your puppy's behavior helps you identify and address any potential issues or challenges that may arise. Whether it's house training, chewing, or separation anxiety, recognizing the underlying causes allows you to implement appropriate strategies and modifications to manage and correct these behaviors effectively.

4. Promoting a Safe and Secure Environment

Understanding your puppy is vital for creating a safe and secure environment. Puppies are naturally curious and can be vulnerable to various dangers if not properly supervised or protected.

- Safety: Understanding your puppy's tendencies and behaviors helps you identify potential hazards within your home or outdoor environment. This includes securing toxic substances, covering electrical cords, and providing safe boundaries to prevent accidents or injuries.

- Health: Recognizing signs of illness or discomfort is essential for prompt veterinary care. Understanding your puppy's normal behavior and physical cues enables you to detect any changes that may indicate an underlying health issue. Early intervention can make a significant difference in their well-being and potentially prevent more serious complications.

5. Nurturing Emotional Well-being

Puppies, like humans, experience a range of emotions. Understanding your puppy's emotional well-being allows you to nurture their happiness and contentment.

- Bonding and Trust: Building a strong connection based on trust and understanding creates a sense of security for your puppy. They rely on you for guidance and comfort, and understanding their emotional needs fosters a deeper bond and trust between you.

- Emotional Support: Just like humans, puppies may experience fear, anxiety, or stress. Understanding their emotional state allows you to provide appropriate support and comfort. Whether it's creating a safe space during thunderstorms or offering reassurance during new experiences, your understanding of their emotional needs can significantly alleviate their distress.

Establishing a Secure and Engaging Surroundings

Creating a secure and engaging environment for your puppy is crucial for their overall well-being and development. Puppies, like children, are curious and energetic creatures, constantly exploring their surroundings. By providing a safe and stimulating environment, you can ensure their physical safety, emotional comfort, and mental enrichment. In this section, we will discuss various aspects of establishing a secure and engaging surrounding for your puppy and offer practical strategies to achieve this goal.

1. Puppy-Proofing Your Home

Before bringing your puppy home, it's essential to puppy-proof your living space. Puppies have a knack for getting into mischief, so taking preemptive measures will help keep them safe.

- Identify Hazards: Take a thorough walk-through of your home and identify potential hazards. Look for items such as toxic plants, cleaning supplies, electrical cords, and small objects that can be choking hazards.

- Secure Dangerous Areas: Some areas, such as the kitchen or laundry room, may contain dangerous substances or appliances. Use baby gates or create physical barriers to restrict your puppy's access to these areas.

- Tidy Up: Keep your living space tidy and organized. Remove clutter, especially objects that your puppy may chew on or knock over, to prevent accidents or injuries.

- Block Off Restricted Areas: If there are specific areas in your home that you want to keep off-limits to your puppy, use baby gates or other barriers to block their access.

2. Providing a Comfortable Living Space

Your puppy needs a comfortable and cozy living space. This space should be their safe haven—a place where they can retreat and feel secure.

- Choose a Dedicated Area: Designate a specific area of your home as your puppy's living space. This can be a room or a corner of a room where their bed, crate, toys, and other essentials are placed.

- Provide a Comfortable Bed: Invest in a comfortable, washable bed for your puppy. Choose a size appropriate for their current and future growth to ensure they have enough space to stretch and relax.

- Create a Sense of Security: Place blankets or clothing with your scent near your puppy's bed to provide comfort and a sense of security. This can help ease any separation anxiety they may experience.

- Temperature and Lighting: Ensure that the temperature in your puppy's living space is comfortable and appropriate for their breed. Avoid exposing them to direct sunlight or drafts that could make them uncomfortable.

Fundamental Care

Providing proper care for your puppy is essential to ensure their health, happiness, and overall well-being. This care encompasses various aspects, including their diet, veterinary care, and grooming. In this section, we will explore the fundamentals of these three crucial areas and discuss practical tips to help you give your puppy the best possible care.

1. Diet and Nutrition

A balanced and nutritious diet is the foundation of good health for your puppy. Proper nutrition supports their growth, development, and overall vitality. Here are some key considerations for your puppy's diet:

- High-Quality Puppy Food:

Select a puppy food which is of good quality and has been specially prepared to fulfill the dietary requirements of young dogs. Look for brands that have undergone rigorous testing and meet the standards set by veterinary nutritionists.

- Age-Appropriate Food:

Select a puppy food that is suitable for your puppy's age and breed size. Different life stages have different nutritional requirements, so ensure that the food is tailored to meet their specific needs.

- Feeding Schedule:

Creating a consistent feeding schedule for your puppy is important.Puppies typically require multiple small meals throughout the day to support their fast metabolism and growth. Consult your veterinarian for guidance on the number of meals and portion sizes appropriate for your puppy's age and breed.

- Portion Control:

Avoid overfeeding your puppy, as excess weight can lead to health issues. Follow the recommended portion sizes provided by the food manufacturer, adjusting as necessary based on your puppy's individual needs and activity level.

- Fresh Water:

Provide fresh and clean water at all times for your puppy. Make sure to change the water frequently to keep it fresh and prevent bacterial growth.

- Treats:

Use treats sparingly and choose healthy options specifically formulated for puppies. Treats should be given as rewards during training or as occasional snacks, but they should not make up a significant portion of your puppy's daily calorie intake.

Remember, each puppy is unique, and their nutritional requirements can differ depending on factors like breed, size, activity level, and health status. It is advisable to seek guidance from your veterinarian to create a customized diet plan that caters to your puppy's specific needs.

2. Veterinary Care

Regular veterinary care is essential to ensure your puppy's health, prevent illness, and address any medical concerns promptly. Here are the important aspects of veterinary care for your puppy:

- Vaccinations:

Vaccinations protect your puppy against common and potentially life-threatening diseases. Follow a vaccination schedule recommended by your veterinarian to ensure your puppy receives all the necessary vaccines at the appropriate times.

- Preventive Medications:

Your veterinarian may recommend preventive medications to protect your puppy from parasites such as fleas, ticks, and heartworms. These medications are crucial for their overall well-being and to prevent the transmission of diseases.

- Wellness Exams:

Schedule regular wellness exams for your puppy, even if they appear healthy. These exams allow the veterinarian to monitor their growth, check for any underlying health issues, and provide preventive care.

- Parasite Screening:

Periodic fecal examinations are essential to check for the presence of intestinal parasites. Early detection and treatment help prevent complications and ensure your puppy's optimal health.

- Spaying/Neutering:

Discuss with your veterinarian the appropriate time to spay or neuter your puppy. This procedure not only prevents unwanted litters but also provides health benefits and reduces the risk of certain diseases.

- Dental Care: Dental hygiene is vital for your puppy's overall health. Regular brushing, dental chews, and dental examinations by a veterinarian help maintain healthy teeth and gums.
- Emergency Care: Familiarize yourself with emergency veterinary clinics in your area. Accidents and illnesses can occur unexpectedly, and having this information readily available can ensure prompt care during emergencies.

3. **Grooming and Hygiene**

Proper grooming practices help keep your puppy clean, comfortable, and free from skin issues. Here are some grooming tips to consider:

- Coat Care:

Brush your puppy's coat regularly to remove loose fur and prevent matting. The frequency of brushing will depend on the length and type of coat your puppy has. Consult your veterinarian or a professional groomer for guidance on the appropriate grooming routine for your puppy's breed.

- Bathing:

Bathe your puppy as needed, using a mild, dog-specific shampoo. Avoid over-bathing, as it can strip the natural oils from their coat and cause dryness or skin irritation. Consult your veterinarian for guidance on the frequency of baths suitable for your puppy's breed and skin type.

- Nail Trimming:

Keep your puppy's nails trimmed to a suitable length. Long nails can cause discomfort and affect their ability to walk properly. If you are unsure how to trim your puppy's nails safely, consult your veterinarian or a professional groomer for assistance.

- Ear Care:

Regularly check your puppy's ears for signs of infection, such as redness, swelling, or a foul odor. Clean their ears as recommended by your veterinarian to prevent ear infections.

- Dental Hygiene:

Begin a dental care routine early by brushing your puppy's teeth regularly with a dog-specific toothbrush and toothpaste. This helps prevent dental diseases and maintains fresh breath.

- Anal Gland Expression:

Some puppies may require anal gland expression to prevent discomfort or infection. Seek guidance from a veterinarian or professional groomer to ensure the safe and appropriate execution of this procedure, as well as to determine when it is necessary to seek professional help.

Remember to approach grooming sessions with patience, gentleness, and positive reinforcement. Make it a positive experience for your puppy to build trust and ensure their comfort during grooming activities.

Variations and Preferences among Dog Breeds

Dog breeds come in a wide variety of sizes, shapes, and temperaments. Each breed has unique characteristics, which often make them well-suited for specific roles and lifestyles. Understanding these variations and preferences among dog breeds can help potential dog owners make informed decisions when choosing a breed that aligns with their lifestyle and preferences.

1. Size and Exercise Needs

Dog breeds vary significantly in terms of size, from tiny toy breeds to large and giant breeds. Along with size, exercise needs differ among breeds as well.

- Toy and Small Breeds: Toy and small breeds, such as Chihuahuas or Shih Tzus, generally require less exercise compared to larger breeds. They are often content with short walks, indoor play, and mental stimulation activities.

- Medium-Sized Breeds: Breeds like Beagles or Border Collies fall into the medium-sized category. They typically require moderate exercise, including daily walks and playtime.

- Large and Giant Breeds: Large and giant breeds, such as Great Danes or Saint Bernards, have higher exercise needs due to their size and energy levels. They benefit from longer walks, off-leash activities, and ample space to run.

It is crucial to consider your own lifestyle and energy levels when choosing a dog breed. If you lead an active lifestyle and have ample time for exercise, a high-energy breed may be a good fit. However, if you prefer a more laid-back lifestyle, a breed with lower exercise requirements may be more suitable.

2. Temperament and Personality Traits

Different dog breeds exhibit various temperament and personality traits. These traits often align with the breed's original purpose and can influence their behavior and compatibility with certain lifestyles.

- Working Breeds: Breeds like German Shepherds or Border Collies were originally bred for working roles, such as herding or guarding. They tend to be intelligent, highly trainable, and thrive when given a job or task to do.

- Sporting Breeds: Breeds like Golden Retrievers or Labrador Retrievers were bred for hunting and retrieving game. They are typically friendly, energetic, and enjoy activities that involve mental and physical stimulation.

- Companion Breeds: Breeds such as Cavalier King Charles Spaniels or Maltese were bred primarily for companionship. They often have affectionate, gentle, and people-oriented personalities, making them well-suited for families or individuals seeking a loyal companion.

- Terrier Breeds: Terrier breeds, like Jack Russell Terriers or Bull Terriers, were bred for hunting and vermin control. They tend to be energetic, feisty, and have a strong prey drive.

Understanding the temperament and personality traits of different breeds can help you choose a dog that aligns with your lifestyle and preferences. If you prefer an independent and self-reliant dog, a working or terrier breed may be a good fit. On the other hand, if you're seeking a highly social and affectionate companion, a companion breed may be more suitable.

3. Coat Types and Grooming Needs

Dog breeds have varying coat types, which result in different grooming requirements.

- Short-Haired Breeds: Breeds like Boxers or Doberman Pinschers have short coats that require minimal grooming. Regular brushing to remove loose hair and occasional bathing are typically sufficient.

- Long-Haired Breeds: Breeds like Shih Tzus or Afghan Hounds have long, flowing coats that require regular brushing and potentially professional grooming to prevent matting and maintain coat health.

- Double-Coated Breeds: Breeds like Siberian Huskies or Alaskan Malamutes have a dense undercoat and a longer outer coat. These breeds often require more frequent brushing and seasonal shedding management.

- Non-Shedding Breeds: Some breeds, such as Poodles or Bichon Frises, have hair that grows continuously and does not shed. These breeds often require regular professional grooming to maintain their coat's health and prevent matting.

Consider your willingness and ability to invest time and effort into grooming when choosing a breed. If you have allergies or prefer a low-maintenance coat, a non-shedding breed may be suitable. However, if you enjoy the grooming process and are willing to devote time to coat care, long-haired breeds may be a good fit.

4. Trainability and Intelligence

Trainability and intelligence levels can vary among different dog breeds. Some breeds are highly trainable and eager to please, while others may be more independent or stubborn.

- Highly Trainable Breeds: Breeds like Border Collies or German Shepherds are known for their high trainability and intelligence. They often excel in obedience training and complex tasks.

- Moderately Trainable Breeds: Breeds like Golden Retrievers or Labrador Retrievers are generally eager to please and respond well to training. They are often used as therapy dogs, search and rescue dogs, or service dogs.

- Independent Breeds: Breeds like Basenjis or Afghan Hounds may have an independent nature and require consistent, patient training methods. They may be more inclined to make their own decisions and require extra effort in training.

When considering trainability, it is essential to remember that every dog is an individual, and training success depends on various factors, including the owner's training approach, consistency, and positive reinforcement methods.

5. Special Considerations: Health and Lifespan

It's important to consider potential health issues and the lifespan associated with different dog breeds. Some breeds may be prone to specific genetic conditions or have shorter or longer lifespans.

- Breed-Specific Health Concerns: Certain breeds have a higher predisposition to specific health issues. For example, large and giant breeds are more prone to orthopedic problems, while some small breeds may be more susceptible to dental issues or respiratory problems.

- Lifespan Variations: Lifespan can vary significantly among different breeds. Smaller breeds generally have longer lifespans, often reaching 10-15 years or more, while larger breeds may have shorter lifespans, averaging 8-12 years.

While it is essential to be mindful of potential health concerns associated with specific breeds, it is equally important to remember that individual health and genetic factors play a significant role. Regular veterinary care, a balanced diet, and proper exercise and grooming practices can contribute to your dog's overall health and lifespan.

Understanding the variations and preferences among dog breeds can assist you in choosing a breed that aligns with your lifestyle, preferences, and capabilities. Size, exercise needs, temperament, coat types, trainability, and health considerations are all factors to consider when selecting a breed. However, it's important to remember that each dog is an individual, and breed traits are generalizations. Taking the time to research and interact with different breeds, as well as seeking guidance from reputable breeders or rescue organizations, can help you make an informed decision and find the perfect companion to enrich your life.

Canine Communication

Communication is a vital aspect of any social species, including dogs. Dogs have their unique ways of expressing themselves and understanding the world around them. Understanding canine communication can help dog owners build stronger bonds with their pets, prevent misunderstandings, and address behavioral issues effectively. Here, we will explore various forms of canine communication and the meanings behind them.

1. Body Language

Body language plays a significant role in canine communication. Dogs use their body postures, facial expressions, and movements to convey their emotions and intentions. Here are some key elements of canine body language:

- Tail Position: The position and movement of a dog's tail can indicate their emotional state. A wagging tail usually signifies happiness or excitement, while a tucked tail suggests fear or submission. A stiff, raised tail can indicate alertness or aggression.

- Ears: The position and movement of a dog's ears also provide important cues. Erect ears signify alertness or curiosity, while flattened ears indicate fear or submission. Some breeds with floppy ears may naturally carry their ears in a relaxed position.

- Body Posture: A dog's overall body posture can convey a range of emotions. A relaxed, loose stance generally indicates contentment, while a tense, rigid posture may suggest aggression or fear. Dogs may also raise their hackles (the hair along the back) when they feel threatened or aroused.

- Facial Expressions: Dogs have expressive faces that can convey various emotions. Dilated pupils may indicate fear or excitement, while narrowed eyes can signal aggression or discomfort. A relaxed, open mouth usually indicates a calm state, while bared teeth or a wrinkled muzzle may suggest aggression.
- Vocalizations: While body language is the primary form of communication, vocalizations also play a role. Dogs use barks, growls, whines, and howls to express different emotions and communicate with other dogs or humans.

It's important to observe and understand a dog's body language in context, considering their overall behavior and the situation they are in. This allows you to interpret their emotions and respond appropriately.

2. Tail Wagging

Tail wagging is often associated with a dog's happiness, but it can convey a range of emotions and intentions. Understanding the nuances of tail wagging is crucial for interpreting a dog's communication accurately. Here are some points to consider:

- Speed and Height: A fast and high tail wag typically indicates excitement, while a slow and low wag may suggest caution or insecurity.
- Direction: The direction of the wag can also provide insights into a dog's emotional state. A wag to the right may indicate positive emotions, such as friendliness or happiness, while a wag to the left may suggest negative emotions or anxiety.
- Stiffness: A stiff, rigid tail accompanied by other signs of tension may indicate aggression or fear, even if there is some wagging present.

It's important to consider the overall context, body language, and the dog's relationship with the person or other dogs when interpreting tail wagging.

3. Vocalizations

Dogs use a variety of vocalizations to communicate, and each vocalization carries a different meaning. Here are some common vocalizations and their possible interpretations:

- Barking: Barking is a versatile vocalization used for various purposes. It can signal excitement, playfulness, alertness, fear, or aggression. The pitch, intensity, and duration of the bark can provide insights into the dog's emotional state.

- Growling: Growling is a warning sign that dogs use to express discomfort, fear, or aggression. It is important to respect a dog's growl as a communication of their boundaries and give them space.

- Whining: Whining is often associated with a dog's desire for attention, comfort, or relief from stress or discomfort. It can also occur when a dog is anxious or in pain.

- Howling: Howling is a form of vocalization used for long-distance communication. Dogs may howl to communicate with other dogs or express their anxiety or distress. Some dogs may also howl in response to certain sounds, such as sirens.

Understanding the context, accompanying body language, and the dog's overall behavior is essential for interpreting vocalizations accurately.

Learn To Recognize What He Feels

As responsible dog owners, it is crucial to be able to recognize and understand what our dogs are feeling. Dogs experience a range of emotions, including fear, pain, happiness, and anxiety, just like humans do. By learning to recognize and interpret their body language and behaviors, we can provide appropriate care and support for our furry friends. In this section, we will explore how to recognize emotions such as fear, pain, and other common feelings in dogs.

1. Fear and Anxiety

Fear and anxiety are common emotions that dogs may experience in various situations. Understanding the signs of fear and anxiety can help you identify when your dog is feeling stressed and take appropriate action. Here are some indicators to look for:

- Body Language: Dogs display several body language cues when they are fearful or anxious. These may include cowering, trembling, pacing, panting excessively, yawning, lip licking, or tucking their tail between their legs. They may also exhibit avoidance behaviors, such as hiding or seeking comfort from their owners.

- Vocalizations: Dogs may vocalize when they are afraid or anxious. This can manifest as whining, whimpering, barking excessively, or growling. Pay attention to the intensity and frequency of vocalizations, as well as any accompanying body language.

- Dilated Pupils: Fear and anxiety can cause a dog's pupils to dilate. If you notice that your dog's eyes appear wider than usual, it may be an indication of heightened stress or fear.

- Aggression: Fear can sometimes lead to aggressive behavior as a defensive response. If your dog shows signs of aggression, such as snapping, growling, or baring teeth, it may be an expression of fear or an attempt to protect themselves.

When your dog is fearful or anxious, it's vital to create a safe and calm environment, provide reassurance, and avoid forcing them into situations that increase their fear. Gradual desensitization and positive reinforcement training can help them overcome their fears and build confidence.

2. Pain and Discomfort

Dogs can experience pain and discomfort due to various reasons, such as injuries, illness, or chronic conditions. Recognizing the signs of pain is essential for providing timely veterinary care and ensuring your dog's well-being. Here are some common indicators of pain:

- Changes in Behavior: Dogs in pain may exhibit changes in their behavior. They may become more withdrawn, lethargic, or irritable. They may also show a decreased interest in activities they typically enjoy.

- Vocalizations: Dogs may vocalize more frequently or in different ways when they are in pain. Whining, whimpering, or yelping can be indicators of discomfort.

- Changes in Appetite: Pain can affect a dog's appetite. They may eat less, show disinterest in their food, or experience difficulty eating or chewing.

- Altered Movement: Dogs in pain may have difficulty moving or display changes in their gait. They may limp, favor certain limbs, or have stiffness in their movements. They may also show reluctance to engage in activities that require physical exertion.

- Body Sensitivity: Dogs in pain may show sensitivity when certain areas of their body are touched or manipulated. They may flinch, growl, or try to avoid contact.

If you suspect that your dog is in pain, it is crucial to consult with a veterinarian to detect the underlying cause and develop an appropriate treatment plan.

3. Happiness and Contentment

Recognizing when your dog is happy and content is equally important for their overall well-being. Here are some signs that indicate your dog is experiencing positive emotions:

- Relaxed Body Language: When a dog is happy and content, their body language is relaxed and loose. Their tail may wag gently, their ears are in their natural position, and their facial expressions appear relaxed.

- Playfulness: Happy dogs often engage in play behavior. They may initiate play with toys, other dogs, or their owners. They may bounce, jump, or have a relaxed and wagging tail during play.

- Appetite and Energy Level: Dogs generally have a healthy appetite and good energy levels when they are happy. They eagerly eat their food, maintain a healthy weight, and have an appropriate level of energy for their age and breed.

- Affectionate Behavior: Happy dogs often seek affection and enjoy being close to their owners. They may lean against you, give gentle nudges, or offer their belly for rubs.
- Contentment and Relaxation: Happy dogs display signs of contentment and relaxation. They may lie down comfortably, take restful naps, and have a soft and relaxed facial expression.

Understanding when your dog is happy and content allows you to reinforce positive behaviors, provide appropriate enrichment and play opportunities, and strengthen your bond with them.

4. Frustration and Boredom

Frustration and boredom can impact a dog's well-being and behavior. Dogs require mental and physical stimulation to prevent boredom and frustration. Here are some signs that may indicate your dog is feeling frustrated or bored:

- Destructive Behavior: Dogs may exhibit destructive behaviors, such as chewing on furniture, excessive digging, or scratching doors and walls when they are bored or frustrated.
- Restlessness: Dogs may become restless and exhibit excessive pacing, circling, or inability to settle down when they are bored or lacking stimulation.
- Attention-Seeking Behavior: Dogs may seek attention through barking, pawing, or nudging when they are bored or seeking stimulation.
- Hyperactivity: Dogs may display hyperactive behavior, including excessive jumping, barking, or running in circles, when they are bored or have excess energy.

To prevent frustration and boredom, provide your dog with regular exercise, mental stimulation through training or puzzle toys, and interactive playtime. Enrichment activities and varied environments can help keep their minds engaged and prevent unwanted behaviors.

2 The Fundamentals Of Canine Instruction

Establishing A Constructive Educational Environment

Establishing an environment that promotes positive learning and enrichment is essential for the development and well-being of your dog. To create such an environment, consider the following steps:

1. **Provide a safe and comfortable space**

Designate a specific area in your home where your dog can feel safe and secure. This could be a crate, a dog bed, or a designated room. Ensure the space is clean, comfortable, and free from any potential hazards.

2. **Set clear boundaries and rules**

Establish clear boundaries and rules for your dog to follow. This helps them understand what behaviors are acceptable and what is not allowed. Consistency is key in enforcing these rules.

3. **Use positive reinforcement**

Positive reinforcement is a powerful technique for training dogs. Reward your dog with praise, treats, and affection whenever they exhibit desired behaviors. This encourages them to repeat those behaviors in the future.

4. **Implement a structured routine**

Dogs do best with a regular schedule. Create a regular schedule that you will follow every day for feeding, exercise, training sessions, and rest. A structured routine helps your dog understand what is expected of them and provides them with a sense of stability.

5. **Engage in regular exercise and mental stimulation**

Physical exercise and mental stimulation are vital for a dog's well-being. Provide regular opportunities for your dog to engage in physical activities like walks, playtime, and interactive toys. Mental stimulation can be achieved through puzzle toys, training exercises, and scent games.

6. Socialize your dog

In order to develop into a balanced canine, socialization is absolutely necessary. Your dog will benefit from having a favorable experience when it is introduced to new people, other animals, and places. This helps them develop good social skills, reduces anxiety, and builds their confidence.

7. Use clear and consistent communication

Dogs understand and respond better to consistent communication. Use clear verbal cues and hand signals for commands and be consistent in your tone and body language. This helps your dog understand what you want from them.

8. Provide appropriate chew toys and outlets for energy

Dogs have a natural instinct to chew. Provide them with a variety of appropriate chew toys to satisfy this need and prevent destructive chewing. Engage in interactive play sessions to help them burn off excess energy.

9. Practice regular training sessions

Regular training sessions help reinforce desired behaviors and establish a bond between you and your dog. Keep training sessions short, focused, and positive. Gradually progress to more challenging commands and behaviors.

Phases Of Growth

The growth of a dog can be divided into several distinct phases, each characterized by specific developmental milestones and needs. Understanding these phases can help you provide appropriate care, training, and socialization for your dog. Let's explore the different phases of growth that dogs typically go through:

1. Neonatal Phase (0-2 weeks)

The neonatal phase begins at birth and lasts until around two weeks of age. During this phase, puppies are completely dependent on their mother for nourishment and warmth. Their eyes and ears are closed, and they spend most of their time sleeping and nursing. They are unable to regulate their body temperature and rely on their mother and littermates for socialization and stimulation.

2. Transitional Phase (2-4 weeks)

Around the age of two weeks, puppies begin to open their eyes and ears, marking the start of the transitional phase. They start to explore their environment, wobble around on unsteady legs, and interact more with their littermates. They also begin to develop their senses and start responding to stimuli in their surroundings.

3. Socialization Phase (3-14 weeks)

The socialization phase is a critical period for a puppy's development. It typically starts around three weeks and extends until around 14 weeks of age. During this phase, puppies are highly receptive to new experiences, people, animals, and environments. It is crucial to expose them to a wide range of positive and supervised experiences to build their confidence, help them develop appropriate social skills, and reduce the likelihood of fear or aggression later in life.

Proper socialization includes introducing puppies to different people, including children, men, women, and individuals with diverse appearances and behaviors. Exposing them to various environments, sounds, surfaces, and objects is also important. Additionally, supervised interactions with other friendly and vaccinated dogs can help develop their social skills.

4. Juvenile Phase (3-6 months)

The juvenile phase is marked by rapid growth and increased energy levels. Puppies become more independent, curious, and playful. They may experience a surge in exploratory behavior and testing boundaries. This is a crucial time for obedience training and reinforcing positive behaviors. Basic commands, such as sit, stay, and come, can be introduced and practiced. Providing mental stimulation, structured exercise, and continued socialization are important during this phase.

5. Adolescent Phase (6-18 months)

The adolescent phase is characterized by hormonal changes and the onset of sexual maturity. Dogs may exhibit behaviors such as increased independence, testing boundaries, and challenging authority. This phase requires continued consistency in training, reinforcement of good behavior, and setting clear boundaries. Patience, positive reinforcement, and ongoing socialization are essential during this stage.

6. Adult Phase (1-3 years)

By the age of one, most dogs are considered adults. However, larger breeds may continue growing and maturing until around the age of three. Dogs in the adult phase have reached their full size and physical development. Training should focus on refining their skills, maintaining good behavior, and providing mental and physical exercise to prevent boredom.

7. Senior Phase (7+ years)

As dogs age, they enter the senior phase of life. This phase varies depending on the size and breed of the dog. Senior dogs may experience physical and cognitive changes, such as reduced mobility, arthritis, or cognitive decline. Adjustments in diet, exercise, and veterinary care are necessary to ensure their well-being and comfort.

It's important to note that the duration and characteristics of each phase may vary among individual dogs. Factors such as breed, genetics, and overall health can influence the pace and development within each stage.

Enclosure Training

Enclosure training, also known as crate training or kennel training, is the process of teaching your dog to feel comfortable and secure in an enclosed space, such as a crate or kennel. This training method has several benefits, including providing a safe and comfortable space for your dog, aiding in housebreaking, and facilitating travel. Let's explore the importance of enclosure training and the steps involved:

Importance of Enclosure Training:
- Safety and Security: An enclosed space provides a safe and secure environment for your dog when you cannot directly supervise them. It prevents them from getting into potentially dangerous situations or causing damage to your home.
- Housebreaking: Enclosure training can aid in housebreaking your dog by teaching them to hold their bladder and bowels. Dogs have a natural instinct to keep their sleeping area clean, so by keeping them in an appropriately sized enclosure, you can encourage them to wait until they're outside to relieve themselves.
- Travel and Vet Visits: Dogs who are accustomed to being in an enclosure are more comfortable during travel or visits to the veterinarian. A familiar and secure space can help reduce anxiety and stress.
- Behavioral Management: Enclosure training can help manage certain behavioral issues, like excessive barking, destructive chewing, or separation anxiety. It provides a controlled space where your dog can relax and feel secure.

Steps for Enclosure Training:

1. Choose the Right Enclosure: Select an appropriate-sized crate or kennel that allows your dog to stand, turn around, and lie down comfortably. It should be well-ventilated and have a secure door.

2. Introduce the Enclosure Gradually: Start by introducing the enclosure as a positive and inviting space. Place soft bedding, toys, and treats inside to create a positive association. Leave the door open initially, allowing your dog to explore at their own pace.

3. Encourage Positive Associations: To help your dog associate the enclosure with positive experiences, feed them meals near or inside the enclosure. Gradually move the food bowls closer to the back of the enclosure to encourage them to spend more time inside.

4. Use Positive Reinforcement: When your dog voluntarily enters the enclosure, praise and reward them with treats or verbal praise. Repeat this process multiple times throughout the day, gradually increasing the duration of time they spend inside.

5. Close the Door: Once your dog is comfortable entering the enclosure, begin closing the door for short periods while they are inside. Stay nearby and offer reassurance. Gradually increase the duration, always ensuring your dog remains calm and comfortable.

6. Extend Enclosure Time: Gradually increase the time your dog spends in the enclosure, both when you are home and when you need to leave. Provide interactive toys or puzzle feeders to keep them mentally stimulated during longer periods of confinement.

7. Never Use the Enclosure for Punishment: It is crucial to maintain a positive association with the enclosure. Never use it as a form of punishment or isolation. The goal is to create a safe and comfortable space that your dog willingly enters.

8. Gradual Independence: Once your dog is comfortable being enclosed, gradually increase their independence. Start by leaving the room for short periods and gradually extend the duration. Always return calmly and avoid making a fuss when leaving or returning.

Be patient, consistent, and ensure that the enclosure is a positive and inviting space for your dog. With proper training and positive reinforcement, your dog can view their enclosure as a safe haven and a valuable tool in their daily routine.

Food Training

Food training, also known as treat training or positive reinforcement training, is a widespread and effective method of teaching dogs new behaviors and reinforcing desired actions. This training technique uses food rewards to motivate and encourage dogs to learn and respond to commands. Food training can be applied to basic obedience commands, complex tricks, and behavior modification. Let's explore the importance of food training and some steps to effectively implement it:

Importance of Food Training:
- Motivation: Food is a powerful motivator for most dogs. By using food rewards during training, you tap into their natural instinct to seek and consume food, which increases their motivation to learn and perform desired behaviors.
- Positive Reinforcement: Food training relies on positive reinforcement, which involves rewarding your dog for exhibiting desired behaviors. This positive association helps strengthen the behavior and encourages your dog to repeat it in the future.

- Clear Communication: Food rewards provide immediate feedback to your dog, signaling that they have done something right. This clear communication helps them understand which behaviors are rewarded and reinforces their understanding of the desired command or action.

Steps for Food Training:

1. Choose High-Value Treats: Select treats that are highly palatable and appealing to your dog. Soft treats that can be easily broken into small pieces are ideal. Use treats that your dog finds especially enticing and reserve them exclusively for training sessions to maintain their value.

2. Start with Basic Commands: Begin food training by teaching your dog simple commands like "sit," "stay," or "come." Hold a treat close to their nose, then gradually move it upward or backward, depending on the command. As their body follows the treat, they naturally assume the desired position. Reward them immediately with the treat and verbal praise. Repeat the process, gradually reducing the frequency of treats as your dog becomes proficient.

3. Shape Behavior: Food training can also be used to shape more complex behaviors. Break down the desired behavior into smaller steps and reward your dog for each successive approximation toward the final behavior. For instance, if you want your dog to learn how to turn over, you should first praise them when they lie down, then again when they move their weight to the side, and ultimately when they finish the roll completely.

4. Capture and Mark Good Behavior: Watch for spontaneous instances of desirable behavior and "capture" them by immediately rewarding your dog with a treat and positive reinforcement. For instance, if your dog sits without being prompted, reward them to reinforce the behavior. Additionally, use a clicker or a verbal marker, such as "yes" or "good," to mark the precise moment your dog performs the desired behavior, signaling that a treat is coming.

5. Fade Treat Dependency: Gradually reduce the frequency of treat rewards as your dog becomes more proficient in performing the desired behaviors. Randomize the delivery of treats, providing them intermittently rather than every time. Replace treats with verbal praise, physical affection, or access to a favorite toy as occasional rewards.

6. Generalize the Training: Practice food training in different environments, with varying distractions and levels of difficulty. Start in a quiet and familiar setting, then gradually introduce distractions such as other people, animals, or noises. This helps your dog generalize their training and respond to commands under different circumstances.

7. Use Food as a Training Tool, Not a Bribe: It's important to transition from using food as a lure to using it as a reward. Once your dog understands the command, gradually phase out the visible presence of the treat during the training session. However, continue to reinforce the behavior intermittently with treats, even if they are not visible initially, to maintain and strengthen the learned behavior.

8. Maintain Consistency: Consistency is key in food training. Use clear, consistent commands and reward your dog promptly and consistently when they exhibit the desired behavior. Avoid confusing your dog by using different commands or inconsistently rewarding behaviors.

Toilet Training

Toilet training, also known as housebreaking or potty training, is an essential aspect of owning a dog. It involves teaching your dog where and when it is appropriate to relieve themselves. Consistency, patience, and positive reinforcement are vital factors in successful toilet training. Let's discuss the importance of toilet training and outline the steps involved:

Importance of Toilet Training:

- Hygiene and Cleanliness: Toilet training ensures that your dog understands where they should eliminate, which helps maintain a clean and hygienic living environment for both you and your pet.

- Convenience: When your dog is toilet trained, you won't have to constantly clean up accidents or worry about them eliminating in inappropriate places. It saves you time and effort in the long run.

- Bonding and Communication: Toilet training provides an opportunity for you to establish a clear line of communication with your dog. It helps strengthen your bond as you work together towards a common understanding.

Steps for Toilet Training:

1. Establish a Routine: Set a consistent routine for your dog's feeding, exercise, and toilet breaks. Dogs generally need to eliminate shortly after eating, waking up from a nap, or engaging in vigorous activity. By establishing a schedule, you can anticipate when your dog will likely need to go outside.

2. Choose a Designated Toilet Area: Select a specific spot outside where you want your dog to eliminate. Take them to this spot consistently to create an association between the area and the act of elimination. The scent left behind will also serve as a reminder for future trips.

3. Supervise and Monitor: Keep a close eye on your dog, especially during the initial stages of toilet training. Supervision allows you to recognize signs that they need to

eliminate, such as sniffing, circling, or restlessness. When you observe these signs, promptly take them to the designated toilet area.

4. Use Verbal Cues: Introduce a specific command or phrase that you can associate with the act of elimination. For example, say "go potty" or "do your business" consistently each time you take your dog to the designated area. This verbal cue will eventually signal to your dog what is expected of them.

5. Reward Successful Elimination: As soon as your dog eliminates in the appropriate area, immediately praise and reward them. Use verbal praise, gentle petting, and small treats to reinforce the desired behavior. Positive reinforcement helps your dog understand that eliminating in the designated area is a positive and rewarding experience.

6. Prevent Accidents: During the initial stages of toilet training, it's important to prevent accidents inside the house. Supervise your dog closely, confine them to a small area, or use a crate or playpen when you cannot directly supervise them. This limits their access to areas where accidents may occur.

7. Clean Accidents Properly: If your dog has an accident indoors, clean the area thoroughly with an enzymatic cleaner specifically designed for pet messes. Avoid using ammonia-based cleaners, as they can leave a scent that may encourage your dog to eliminate in the same spot again.

8. Be Patient and Consistent: Toilet training takes time and patience. Consistency is crucial in reinforcing the desired behavior. Stick to the routine, take your dog outside regularly, and continue to praise and reward them for eliminating in the appropriate area. Avoid punishment or scolding, as it can create fear and confusion.

9. Gradually Extend Time Between Breaks: As your dog becomes more reliable in their toilet training, gradually increase the time between bathroom breaks. Extend the intervals based on their age, breed, and ability to hold their bladder. However, be mindful not to stretch the duration too quickly, as it may result in accidents.

10. Maintain a Routine: Even after your dog is fully toilet trained, maintaining a consistent routine is important. Continue to provide regular opportunities for them to eliminate outside and reinforce the desired behavior with praise and rewards.

Progressive Training

Progressive training, also known as progressive reinforcement training or positive reinforcement training, is an approach to dog training that focuses on using positive reinforcement techniques to teach desired behaviors and modify unwanted behaviors. It is predicated on the idea that the dog and its owner should develop a close relationship characterized by trust and mutual respect for one another. Progressive training involves gradually increasing the level of difficulty and complexity of the training tasks as the dog learns and progresses. Here are some benefits of progressive training:

- Positive Reinforcement: Progressive training relies heavily on positive reinforcement, which involves rewarding desired behaviors with praise, treats, toys, or other rewards that the dog finds motivating. This approach encourages dogs to repeat the desired behaviors in order to receive the rewards, making the learning process enjoyable and engaging.

- Clear Communication: Progressive training emphasizes clear and effective communication between the dog and the owner. It involves using consistent verbal cues, hand signals, and body language to convey commands and expectations. This helps the dog understand what is being asked of them and reduces confusion or frustration.

- Step-by-Step Progression: Progressive training follows a gradual progression of training tasks, starting with simple and easy behaviors and gradually building up to more complex behaviors. This allows the dog to understand and master each step before moving on to the next, ensuring a solid foundation of learning and success.

- Patience and Flexibility: Progressive training requires patience and flexibility from the owner. Each dog learns at their own pace, so it's important to be patient and provide ample time for the dog to understand and respond to the training cues. Additionally, being flexible and adjusting the training approach based on the individual dog's needs and learning style can greatly enhance the effectiveness of the training.

- Problem Solving and Adaptability: Progressive training encourages problem-solving and adaptability from both the dog and the owner. It involves identifying and addressing any challenges or obstacles that may arise during the training process. By adapting the training methods or breaking down the behavior into smaller steps, both the dog and the owner can work together to overcome difficulties and achieve success.

- Strengthening the Human-Dog Bond: Progressive training fosters a strong bond and trust between the dog and the owner. The positive reinforcement techniques used in progressive training create a positive and rewarding association with training sessions, making the dog more willing to engage and cooperate. This deepens the connection and strengthens the relationship between the dog and the owner.

- Promoting Lifelong Learning: Progressive training promotes ongoing learning and enrichment for the dog. Once basic obedience commands are mastered, it opens the door to more advanced training, such as trick training, agility, or other specialized activities. This continual learning keeps the dog mentally stimulated, happy, and engaged throughout their life.

Socialization Training

Socialization training involves exposing your dog to various people, animals, environments, and experiences in a positive and controlled manner. The primary goal of socialization training is to help your dog develop appropriate social skills, reduce fear or aggression towards new stimuli, and increase their overall confidence in different situations.

Why is Socialization Training Important?

- Behavior Development: Early socialization plays a significant role in shaping your dog's behavior and temperament. Properly socialized dogs are more likely to exhibit friendly and confident behaviors towards unfamiliar people, animals, and environments.

- Fear and Aggression Prevention: Socialization training helps prevent fear-based behaviors and aggression. By exposing your dog to a wide range of stimuli in a positive and controlled manner, you can reduce their fear response and build their confidence.

- Adaptability: Dogs that are well-socialized adapt better to new situations, environments, and changes in routine. They are more comfortable and relaxed in various settings, which makes them easier to handle and less likely to develop anxiety or stress-related issues.

- Safety: Socialization training teaches your dog appropriate behavior around people and other animals, reducing the risk of aggressive reactions or unpredictable behavior. It promotes safe interactions and helps prevent incidents in public or social settings.

Steps for Socialization Training:

1. Early Start: Begin socialization training as early as possible, ideally when your dog is between 3 and 14 weeks old. This period, known as the "critical socialization period," is when puppies are most receptive to new experiences and learning.

2. Positive Exposure to People: Expose your dog to a variety of people of different ages, genders, and ethnicities. Encourage positive interactions by asking strangers to offer treats, praise, or gentle petting. Gradually expose your dog to people wearing hats, sunglasses, or other accessories to help them become accustomed to different appearances.

3. Introduce Other Animals: Expose your dog to well-behaved and vaccinated dogs of different sizes, breeds, and temperaments. Start with controlled interactions in a neutral environment, such as a supervised puppy class or a friend's dog. Gradually increase the complexity of the interactions, monitoring body language and ensuring positive experiences.

4. Explore Different Environments: Your dog should be taken to a variety of different places, including parks, streets, beaches, crowded areas, and calmer settings. Begin in places with lower levels of stimulation and work your way up to more intense stimulation over time. Introduce them to common sights and sounds, such as traffic, bicycles, strollers, and loud noises, in a controlled manner to help them become more comfortable.

5. Positive Reinforcement: During socialization training, use positive reinforcement techniques to reward your dog for calm and relaxed behavior in new situations. Praise, treats, and toys can be used to create positive associations and reinforce appropriate responses.

6. Controlled Experiences: Ensure that all socialization experiences are controlled and safe. Use a leash and harness to maintain control during interactions and gradually increase off-leash experiences as your dog's social skills improve. Avoid

overwhelming or traumatic experiences that could have a negative impact on their confidence.

7. Gradual Exposure: Introduce new experiences and stimuli gradually, considering your dog's comfort level and individual temperament. Monitor their body language for signs of stress or fear, such as cowering, trembling, or excessive panting. If your dog shows signs of distress, take a step back and reintroduce the stimulus at a slower pace or from a greater distance.

8. Ongoing Socialization: Socialization training should be an ongoing process throughout your dog's life. Continue to expose them to new experiences, environments, and interactions. Regularly engage in controlled playdates, visit dog-friendly locations, and participate in training classes or activities that involve social interactions.

Agility Training

Agility training is a fun and physically stimulating activity for dogs that involves navigating through a course of obstacles. It enhances their physical fitness, mental agility, and strengthens the bond between the dog and the handler. Here is a step-by-step guide for agility training with your dog:

1. Assess Your Dog's Fitness and Health: Before starting agility training, ensure that your dog is in good health and physically fit for the activity. Consult with your veterinarian to ensure your dog is free from any underlying health issues that may affect their ability to participate in agility training.

2. Basic Obedience Training: Begin by establishing a solid foundation of basic obedience training. Your dog should have a good understanding of commands such

as sit, stay, come, and lie down. This will help with control and communication during agility training.

3. Introduce Basic Equipment: Start with introducing basic agility equipment such as tunnels and low jumps. Encourage your dog to explore and interact with these obstacles using positive reinforcement techniques. Use treats, praise, and toys as rewards for successfully navigating the equipment.

4. Target Training: Teach your dog to target specific objects, such as a target stick or a contact zone on an agility obstacle. This helps in directing their focus and teaches them to follow your cues and instructions.

5. Introduce Weave Poles: Gradually introduce weave poles to your dog. Begin with just a few poles and use treats or toys to guide them through the poles. Increase the number of poles as your dog becomes more confident and proficient in weaving.

6. Teach Contacts: Train your dog to perform contacts on obstacles such as the A-frame, dog walk, and teeter-totter. Teach them to touch specific areas on the contact zones with their paws, reinforcing the behavior with treats and praise.

7. Introduce Jumps and Hurdles: Gradually increase the height and complexity of jumps and hurdles. Start with low jumps and gradually raise the height as your dog becomes more comfortable and proficient. Use positive reinforcement to encourage your dog to clear the jumps with confidence.

8. Introduce Tunnels and Chutes: Introduce tunnels and chutes to your dog, gradually building their confidence to enter and navigate through them. Use treats or toys to motivate them to move through the tunnels, gradually increasing the length and complexity of the tunnels.

9. String Obstacles Together: Start stringing multiple obstacles together to create a mini-agility course. Begin with a simple sequence and gradually increase the complexity as your dog becomes more skilled. Use verbal cues and hand signals to guide your dog through the course.

10. Practice and Refine Skills: Regularly practice the different agility obstacles and sequences with your dog. Focus on refining their skills, improving their speed, accuracy, and responsiveness to your commands. Be patient and encourage your dog with positive reinforcement throughout the training process.

11. Participate in Agility Classes or Competitions: Consider enrolling in agility classes or participating in local agility competitions. These opportunities provide a structured environment for your dog to showcase their agility skills and further their training.

Remember to always prioritize your dog's safety during agility training. Ensure that the equipment is safe and properly set up, and monitor your dog for any signs of fatigue or discomfort. Keep training sessions fun, short, and engaging to maintain your dog's enthusiasm.

Agility training is a progressive process, and each dog learns at their own pace. Be patient, celebrate small achievements, and enjoy the journey of training and bonding with your dog through agility.

Behavioral Adjustment

Behavioral adjustment in dogs refers to the process of modifying or changing a dog's behavior to achieve a desired outcome or address problematic behaviors. It involves using various training techniques and methods to shape the dog's behavior and encourage positive, appropriate responses. Here are somecommon behavioral issues that dogs may exhibit, along with a brief description of each issue and steps to address and adjust these behaviors:

1. Separation Anxiety

Dogs with separation anxiety become distressed when separated from their owners and may exhibit behaviors like excessive barking, destructive chewing, or house soiling.
Steps to Solve:

- Gradually desensitize your dog to being alone by practicing short absences.
- Create a calm and comfortable environment for your dog when you're away.
- Provide interactive toys or puzzle feeders to keep them occupied.
- Consider professional help from a dog behaviorist for severe cases.

2. Excessive Barking

Dogs may bark excessively due to boredom, fear, or territoriality, which can be disruptive and annoying. Steps to Solve:

- Identify the triggers for barking and address the underlying cause.
- Provide mental and physical stimulation to prevent boredom.
- Teach the "quiet" command using positive reinforcement.
- Use distraction techniques or redirect your dog's focus when barking excessively.

3. Leash Pulling

Dogs may pull on the leash, making walks unpleasant and difficult to manage.
Steps to Solve:

- Use positive reinforcement to reward loose leash walking.
- Teach your dog to pay attention to you by using verbal cues or treats.
- Use a front-clip harness or head collar to discourage pulling.
- Practice regular leash training sessions and gradually increase distractions.

4. Jumping on People

Dogs may jump on people as a way to greet or seek attention, which can be overwhelming and unwanted.

Steps to Solve:

- Ignore the behavior and avoid eye contact or physical interaction.
- Teach an alternative behavior, such as sitting or offering a paw for greeting.
- Reward your dog for keeping all four paws on the ground.
- Practice consistent training and reinforce boundaries with visitors.

5. Destructive Chewing

Dogs may chew on inappropriate items, such as furniture or shoes, which can be destructive and costly.

Steps to Solve:

- Provide appropriate chew toys to redirect their chewing behavior.
- Puppy-proof your home by keeping valuable or dangerous items out of reach.
- Supervise your dog and interrupt inappropriate chewing with a firm "no."
- Use deterrent sprays or bitter-tasting substances on items you want to protect.

6. Digging

Dogs may dig out of boredom, to escape confinement, or as a natural instinct.

Steps to Solve:

- Provide alternative outlets for natural digging behavior, such as a designated digging area or a sandbox.
- Increase exercise and mental stimulation to alleviate boredom.
- Reinforce boundaries and limit access to areas where digging is problematic.

- Consider environmental modifications, such as burying rocks or chicken wire to discourage digging.

7. Counter Surfing

Dogs may jump on countertops or tables to steal food or items, which can be dangerous and unhygienic.

Steps to Solve:

- Remove any tempting items or food from the dog's reach.
- Use deterrents, such as aluminum foil or motion-activated devices, to discourage counter surfing.
- Teach the "leave it" and "off" commands to redirect your dog's attention.
- Provide appropriate food and enrichment options to prevent boredom and reduce the motivation to counter surf.

8. Excessive Energy and Hyperactivity

Dogs with excessive energy and hyperactivity may struggle to relax, focus, and engage in appropriate behaviors.

Steps to Solve:

- Increase physical exercise to help drain excess energy.
- Provide mental stimulation through puzzle toys, training sessions, or interactive games.
- Establish a consistent routine and provide structure to your dog's day.
- Teach and reinforce calm behaviors, such as settling on a mat or in a designated area.

Training Mature Dogs

Training mature dogs can be a rewarding experience, although it may require some extra patience and understanding compared to training puppies. Here are some steps you can follow to train a mature dog:

1. Set realistic expectations: Understand that older dogs may have ingrained habits or behaviors that will take time and consistency to modify. Be patient and maintain a positive attitude throughout the training process.

2. Establish a routine: Establishing a daily regimen that includes feeding, exercise, and training sessions is beneficial for dogs since they thrive on predictability. This predictability helps them understand what is expected of them and reduces confusion.

3. Use positive reinforcement: Implementing positive reinforcement is highly recommended as it is widely recognized as the most effective and humane training method for dogs. Reward your dog with treats, praise, or play whenever they exhibit the desired behavior. This encourages them to repeat the behavior in the future.

4. Identify specific training goals: Determine what behaviors you want to teach or modify in your mature dog. Break these goals down into small, achievable steps, and focus on one behavior at a time. For example, if you want to teach them to sit, start by rewarding them for simply bending their legs and gradually progress to a full sit.

5. Start with basic obedience commands: Begin training with basic obedience commands such as sit, stay, come, and lie down. Use consistent verbal cues and hand signals to help your dog understand what you want them to do.

6. Be consistent: Consistency is crucial when training a mature dog. Use the same commands, rewards, and techniques every time. Avoid confusing your dog by sending mixed signals or changing the rules.

7. Practice short but frequent training sessions: Older dogs may have shorter attention spans, so keep training sessions brief and engaging. Aim for multiple short sessions throughout the day rather than one long session. This helps maintain their focus and prevents them from becoming bored or frustrated.

8. Socialize your dog: If your mature dog lacks social skills or displays behavioral issues around other dogs or people, consider socialization training. Gradually expose them to new environments, situations, and individuals in a controlled and positive manner. Seek the assistance of a skilled dog trainer if needed.

9. Manage and prevent unwanted behaviors: During training, manage your dog's environment to prevent them from engaging in unwanted behaviors. For example, if your dog has a habit of counter surfing, remove food from accessible areas or use baby gates to restrict access to certain rooms.

10. Be patient and persistent: Remember that training a mature dog takes time and patience. Celebrate small victories and don't get discouraged by setbacks. With consistent training and positive reinforcement, you can help your mature dog learn new behaviors and overcome any challenges.

Essential Commands Your Dog Should Learn For Obedience

When it comes to obedience training, there are several essential commands that can greatly improve your dog's behavior and ensure their safety. Here are some important commands that your dog should learn:

Sit:

Teaching your dog to sit on command is one of the basic and most important commands. It helps control impulsive behavior, keeps them calm, and is useful in various situations.

Steps:

1. You should start by raising your hand gradually over your dog's head while holding a little goodie close to their nose. As their nose moves toward the treat, they should find themselves falling into a seated position on their own accord.

2. When they are in the seated position, you should tell them to "sit" and then present them with the reward while also giving them applause.

3. Carry through this procedure a number of times, progressively incorporating the verbal cue "sit" prior to you employ the hand gesture.

4. Eventually, phase out the treat, but continue to praise and reward your dog for sitting on command.

Stay:

The "stay" command teaches your dog to remain in a specific position until given a release cue. This command is crucial for their safety, especially in situations where they may encounter potential dangers.

Steps:

1. Start with your dog in a sitting or lying down position.

2. With an open hand, palm facing towards your dog, say "stay" in a strong but calm voice.

3. Move a step backwards whilst keeping eye contact with your dog the entire time. If they stay in place, immediately return to them and reward them with praise and a treat.

4. Slowly expand both the distance traveled and the length of time spent there, always returning to your dog to reward them before releasing them from the stay.

Come:

Teaching your dog to come when called is vital for their safety and allows you to maintain control in various situations. It's important to reinforce a strong recall response.

Steps:

1. Begin in a low-distraction environment such as your home or backyard.

2. Crouch down and open your arms while excitedly calling your dog's name followed by "come" (e.g., "Buddy, come!").

3. When your dog comes to you, reward them with praise, treats, and affection.

4. Gradually introduce more distractions and practice the "come" command in different environments, always rewarding your dog when they respond correctly.

Lie Down:

The "lie down" command is useful for settling your dog, controlling their excitement, and promoting relaxation. It can be particularly helpful in situations where you need them to stay calm and focused.

Steps:

1. Start with your dog in a sitting position.

2. Hold a treat in your closed fist near their nose, then lower your hand to the ground in front of them.

3. As your dog follows the treat with their nose, they should naturally lower their body into a lying down position.

4. Once they are lying down, say "lie down" and reward them with the treat and praise.

5. Practice this command repeatedly, gradually phasing out the treat while continuing to reward them with praise and affection.

Leave It:

The "leave it" command teaches your dog to ignore or move away from something they find interesting or potentially dangerous. This command is essential for preventing them from picking up harmful objects or approaching hazardous situations.

Steps:

1. Hold a treat in your closed fist and present it to your dog, saying "leave it" in a firm tone.

2. Whenzyour dog stops trying to get the treat from your hand, even for a moment, immediately reward them with a different treat from your other hand or from a nearby source.

3. Repeat this process, gradually increasing the time duration before rewarding and using a variety of objects or treats as distractions.

4. Extend the command to objects on the ground or other areas, always reinforcing the "leave it" command with a reward when your dog complies.

Off:

Teaching your dog to get off furniture, people, or objects is important for their safety and ensures they understand appropriate boundaries.

Steps:

1. When your dog is jumping up on people or furniture, firmly say "off" in a calm but assertive tone.

2. Gently guide your dog off the person or furniture and onto the ground.

3. Once they are off, reward them with praise and attention.

4. Consistently use the command "off" whenever your dog attempts to jump up, and reward them when they respond correctly.

Touch:

The "touch" command is crucial for teaching your dog to target their nose to your hand, allowing for guided movements during playtime and other activities.

Steps:

1. Present your open palm to your dog at their nose level.

2. Say "touch" in a clear and encouraging voice.

3. When your dog touches their nose to your palm, immediately reward them with a treat and praise.

4. Repeat this process several times, gradually moving your palm to different positions.

5. Once your dog understands the command, introduce different surfaces or objects for them to touch, such as a target stick or a specific part of your body.

6. Practice the "touch" command during playtime by incorporating it into games that require your dog to follow your hand or target specific objects.

3

The Significance Of Play And Activity For Canines

Engaging in Playtime with Dogs for their Well-being and Cognitive Development

Engaging in playtime with dogs is not only a fun and enjoyable activity but also plays a crucial role in their overall well-being and cognitive development. Playtime offers numerous benefits for dogs, both physically and mentally.

Play serves as a natural outlet for dogs to expend their energy, exercise their bodies, and maintain physical fitness. Through play, dogs engage in various movements such as running, jumping, fetching, and wrestling, which promote cardiovascular health, muscle development, and overall agility. Regular play sessions help prevent obesity, improve coordination, and enhance their overall physical condition. Additionally, physical activity during play releases endorphins, known as the "feel-good" hormones, which promote relaxation, reduce stress, and contribute to a positive emotional state.

Moreover, playtime serves as a valuable social interaction for dogs. Dogs are social animals, and play provides them with opportunities to socialize with humans, other dogs, and even other species. Interacting with others during play helps dogs develop important social skills, such as bite inhibition, appropriate play behaviors, and understanding of social cues. Through play, dogs learn to communicate effectively, establish and maintain social bonds, and develop a sense of belonging within their social groups. These social interactions during play contribute to their overall mental and emotional well-being.

In addition to physical and social benefits, playtime significantly impacts a dog's cognitive development. Dogs are intelligent animals with a natural curiosity and problem-solving abilities. Engaging in play stimulates their minds, promotes mental agility, and enhances their cognitive functions. Let's explore some specific ways in which play contributes to a dog's cognitive development:

- Problem-solving skills: Certain play activities, such as puzzle toys or interactive games, require dogs to use their problem-solving abilities to access treats or toys. This stimulates their cognitive processes, encourages critical thinking, and enhances their ability to find creative solutions.

- Focus and concentration: Play sessions that involve training games or activities that require dogs to follow instructions enhance their focus and concentration. Dogs learn to pay attention, listen to cues, and respond appropriately, which strengthens their cognitive abilities and improves their overall trainability.

- Memory and learning: Engaging in playtime that involves learning new tricks or commands helps dogs develop their memory and learning skills. Dogs remember the cues, associate them with specific actions, and retain the knowledge gained through play.

- Sensory stimulation: Play engages a dog's senses, including sight, smell, hearing, and touch. Different types of toys, textures, and environments stimulate their sensory perception, which enhances their cognitive abilities and helps them make sense of the world around them.

- Emotional intelligence: Playtime also plays a role in developing a dog's emotional intelligence. Through play, dogs learn to interpret and respond to various emotional cues, both from humans and other dogs. This understanding of emotions fosters empathy, enhances their ability to form social bonds, and contributes to their overall emotional well-being.

It's important to note that play should be tailored to suit each dog's individual needs, preferences, and physical capabilities. Some dogs may enjoy active play sessions with toys, balls, and running, while others may prefer mentally stimulating games or interactive puzzles. The key is to provide a variety of play activities that engage their minds and bodies.

Essential Guidelines for Carefree Playtime

To make the most out of playtime with your dog, here are some tips:

1. **Choose a suitable play area**

Select a secure and appropriate space for play. If indoors, clear away any fragile or valuable items that could be knocked over or damaged. If outdoors, ensure the area is fenced or free from potential hazards.

2. **Use safe and durable toys**

Opt for toys that are specifically designed for dogs and are safe for them to chew on or play with. Avoid small toys or those with detachable parts that could be swallowed or pose a choking hazard.

3. **Supervise play sessions**

Always supervise your dog during playtime, especially when introducing new toys or engaging in interactive games. This allows you to monitor their behavior, intervene if necessary, and ensure a safe play environment.

4. **Match play intensity with your dog's energy level**

Adjust the intensity of play to match your dog's energy level. High-energy dogs may enjoy more active play, such as fetching or tug-of-war, while calmer dogs may prefer gentler activities like puzzle toys or hide-and-seek.

5. **Take breaks and avoid overexertion**

Dogs can become easily overexcited during play, leading to exhaustion or potential injuries. Take periodic breaks and provide water to prevent dehydration. If your dog appears tired or panting excessively, it's time to rest.

6. Teach and reinforce appropriate play behavior

Use playtime as an opportunity to reinforce good behavior and discourage undesirable habits. Reward your dog for playing gently, following commands, or releasing toys on cue. Redirect them if they become too rough or exhibit inappropriate behavior.

7. Avoid rough play and encourage self-control

While some dogs enjoy rough-and-tumble play, it's important to establish boundaries and discourage aggressive behavior. Teach your dog to control their impulses, practice self-restraint, and respond to cues for gentle play.

8. Respect your dog's signals and limits

Dogs communicate through body language. Respect their signals and cues during play. If your dog shows signs of discomfort, fear, or stress, such as freezing, growling, or attempting to hide, immediately stop the activity and provide reassurance.

9. Engage in interactive play and bonding

Playtime is an excellent opportunity to strengthen your bond with your dog. Engage in interactive play, such as fetch or hide-and-seek, where you actively participate. This not only provides mental stimulation but also deepens your connection.

10. End play on a positive note

Finish play sessions on a positive and calm note. Gradually wind down the activity, offer praise or treats, and provide your dog with a chance to relax and recover. This helps your dog associate playtime with positive experiences and avoids abrupt transitions.

Encouragement Through Rewards, Not Punishment

Encouragement through rewards, rather than punishment, is a highly effective and humane approach to training and interacting with dogs. This method focuses on positive reinforcement, where desired behaviors are rewarded, leading to increased motivation and willingness to learn.

unishment-based training methods, such as physical corrections or scolding, rely on fear and intimidation to suppress unwanted behaviors. While these techniques may yield short-term results, they can have long-lasting negative effects on a dog's well-being and the human-animal bond.

One major drawback of punishment is its potential to create fear, anxiety, and mistrust in dogs. Dogs that are subjected to punishment may become fearful or defensive, leading to increased aggression, avoidance behaviors, or even shutting down. This not only hinders the learning process but also damages the emotional well-being of the dog.

In contrast, rewards-based training focuses on reinforcing desired behaviors through positive experiences. By rewarding a dog for performing the desired behavior, such as sitting or walking politely on a leash, you motivate them to repeat that behavior in the future. This approach builds trust, strengthens the bond between the dog and their human, and cultivates a positive learning environment.

Implementing encouragement through rewards in your dog training and interactions is both simple and effective. Here are some practical steps to incorporate this approach:

1. Identify desired behaviors: Determine the behaviors you want to reinforce in your dog, such as sitting, lying down, or walking calmly on a leash. Break down complex behaviors into smaller, achievable steps to facilitate learning.

2. Select appropriate rewards: Choose rewards that are meaningful and motivating for your dog. Food treats, praise, petting, or playtime are commonly used rewards. Use high-value treats for more challenging behaviors or in distracting environments.

3. Timing is crucial: Deliver the reward immediately after your dog performs the desired behavior. This helps them associate the reward with the specific action they just performed, reinforcing the connection between the behavior and the reward.

4. Be consistent: Consistency is key in positive reinforcement training. Reinforce the desired behavior every time it occurs, at least during the initial stages of training. This helps your dog understand the association between the behavior and the reward.

5. Use verbal and visual cues: Pair verbal cues, such as "sit" or "down," with the desired behavior. Over time, your dog will associate these cues with the corresponding action. You can also use hand signals or gestures to enhance communication.

6. Gradually reduce rewards: Once a behavior is reliably performed, gradually reduce the frequency of rewards. Transition to intermittent reinforcement, where the dog is rewarded randomly for the behavior, to maintain its strength.

7. Avoid punishment and negative reinforcement: Refrain from using punishment or negative reinforcement techniques, such as physical corrections or yelling. Instead, redirect your dog's focus to the desired behavior and reward them when they comply.

Training Tips

Start with Basic Commands:

Teaching your dog fundamental commands like sit, stay, and come serves multiple purposes. Not only does it establish clear communication between you and your dog, but it also provides valuable mental stimulation. These commands engage your dog's cognitive abilities, promote focus, and encourage obedience. Begin with short training sessions, gradually increasing the duration as your dog becomes more adept.

Incorporate Scent Work:

Dogs have an incredible sense of smell, and engaging their noses in scent work exercises can be highly stimulating. You can play games like hiding treats or toys around the house and encouraging your dog to find them using their sense of smell. You can also try introducing them to the sport of nosework, where they search for specific scents in various environments.

Puzzle Toys and Treat Dispensers:

Puzzle toys and treat dispensers are excellent tools for mental stimulation. These toys require your dog to problem-solve and use their intelligence to access the treats or solve the puzzle. There are a variety of puzzle toys available, from ones that require your dog to move pieces to others that dispense treats when manipulated correctly. Rotate different toys to keep the challenge level high and maintain your dog's interest.

Teach New Tricks:

Teaching your dog new tricks is a fantastic way to engage their minds and deepen your bond. From simple tricks like "shake hands" or "roll over" to more complex tricks like "play dead" or "fetch a specific toy," the possibilities are endless. Break down the trick into small steps, use positive reinforcement, and be patient. Training sessions should be short and enjoyable for both you and your dog.

Engage in Interactive Play:

Interactive play sessions not only provide physical exercise but also mental stimulation. Games like tug-of-war, hide-and-seek, and fetch can engage your dog's problem-solving abilities and promote mental engagement. Incorporate commands like "sit" or "stay" during playtime to add an extra level of mental challenge.

Training Mistakes

Lack of Consistency:

Consistency is key when it comes to training. Inconsistency can confuse your dog and make it difficult for them to understand what is expected of them. Use the same commands and gestures consistently, and ensure that all family members are on the same page with training methods and rules.

Harsh Training Methods:

Using harsh training methods, such as yelling, physical punishment, or aversive tools, can be detrimental to your dog's mental well-being. Opting for positive reinforcement techniques, such as rewards and praise, proves to be more effective in training and establishes a trusting and positive relationship with your dog. It is essential to concentrate on acknowledging and rewarding desired behaviors rather than resorting to punishment for unwanted ones.

Skipping Basic Training:

Basic training is the foundation for all other training exercises. Skipping or neglecting basic training can lead to behavioral issues and make it challenging to progress to more advanced mental exercises. Invest time in teaching your dog fundamental commands and manners, as they form the building blocks for mental stimulation.

Overlooking Mental Exercise:

Physical exercise is crucial, but don't overlook the importance of mental exercise for your dog. Boredom can lead to destructive behaviors, excessive barking, or anxiety. Incorporating mental exercises into your dog's daily routine helps keep their minds sharp and engaged.

Neglecting Individual Needs:

Every dog is unique, and it's essential to consider their individual needs and preferences when engaging in mental exercises. Some dogs may prefer scent work, while others enjoy problem-solving toys or learning new tricks. Observe and understand what activities your dog enjoys the most, and tailor the mental exercises accordingly.

Toys

Toys are essential for dogs for several reasons:

1. **Mental Stimulation:** Dogs are intelligent creatures that require mental stimulation to prevent boredom and maintain cognitive health. Toys challenge their problem-solving abilities, encourage exploration, and engage their minds in constructive ways.

2. **Physical Exercise:** Many toys promote physical activity, which is crucial for a dog's overall health and well-being. Tug toys, balls, and interactive toys encourage movement, running, jumping, and chasing, helping dogs burn off excess energy and maintain physical fitness.

3. **Emotional Outlet:** Dogs need an outlet for their natural instincts and behaviors. Toys provide a healthy and constructive way for dogs to chew, bite, and manipulate objects, reducing destructive behavior and providing an emotional outlet.

4. **Stress Relief:** Chewing on toys can be a soothing and stress-relieving activity for dogs. It helps alleviate anxiety, promotes relaxation, and provides a sense of comfort and security.

5. **Bonding and Socialization**: Interactive toys can be used to play games with your dog, strengthening the bond between you and providing opportunities for socialization. Playing together with toys enhances communication, trust, and companionship.

Types of Toys:

There is a wide variety of toys available for dogs, each serving a different purpose. Let's explore some common types of toys:

- Chew Toys: Chew toys are designed for dogs to satisfy their natural urge to chew. They help promote dental health by reducing plaque and tartar buildup, relieve teething discomfort in puppies, and redirect chewing behavior from destructive items.

- Interactive Puzzle Toys: Puzzle toys require dogs to solve a problem or manipulate parts to access treats or rewards. These toys stimulate their problem-solving skills, keep them mentally engaged, and provide a challenge.

- Plush Toys: Plush toys are soft and cuddly, providing comfort and companionship to dogs. They are suitable for dogs that enjoy gentle play and may serve as a source of comfort during rest or sleep.

- Balls and Fetch Toys: Balls and fetch toys are excellent for interactive play and physical exercise. Dogs love chasing and retrieving these toys, which provide an outlet for their natural prey drive and promote active engagement.

- Tug Toys: Tug toys are designed for interactive play between dogs and their owners. They can be used for training, building strength, and bonding. It is important to establish clear rules and boundaries during tug-of-war play to prevent any accidental injuries or reinforcement of undesirable behaviors.

- Squeaky Toys: Squeaky toys produce a sound that mimics prey, triggering a dog's instinctual response. They provide entertainment, mental stimulation, and can help redirect chewing or destructive behaviors.

- Treat-Dispensing Toys: These toys are designed to hold treats or kibble, requiring dogs to work for their food. They encourage problem-solving, keep dogs mentally engaged, and slow down eating for fast eaters.

Considerations for Toy Selection:

When choosing toys for your dog, consider the following factors:

- Size and Safety

Select toys appropriate for your dog's size to avoid choking hazards or injuries. Ensure that toys are durable, free from small parts that can be swallowed, and made of non-toxic materials.

- Age and Developmental Stage

Puppies have different toy needs compared to adult dogs. Choose toys suitable for their age and developmental stage. For example, teething puppies may benefit from softer chew toys designed for their needs.

- Individual Preferences

Consider your dog's preferences, play style, and activity level when selecting toys. Some dogs may enjoy chasing and retrieving balls, while others may prefer solving puzzles or playing with plush toys.

- Durability

Look for toys that are designed to withstand your dog's chewing strength and play style. Reinforced stitching, sturdy materials, and durable construction can extend the lifespan of the toy.

- Safety Testing

Check for toys that have undergone safety testing and certification to ensure they meet quality and safety standards. Look for labels indicating that the toy is free from harmful chemicals or substances.

- Supervision

Always supervise your dog during playtime, especially with new toys or toys that can be easily destroyed. Remove any broken or damaged toys to prevent ingestion of small parts.

- Rotation and Variety

Rotate your dog's toys regularly to maintain their interest and prevent boredom. Introduce new toys occasionally to provide novelty and mental stimulation.

- Individual Considerations

Take into account any specific considerations for your dog, such as allergies, sensitivities, or physical limitations. For example, some dogs may have specific dietary restrictions that should be considered when choosing treat-dispensing toys.

Outdoor and Indoor Fun - Enhancing the Fun Factor for Human-Dog Teams

Establishing a strong bond and spending quality time with your beloved furry companion is greatly enhanced by engaging in enjoyable activities. Whether you choose to venture outdoors or opt for indoor play sessions, these experiences offer valuable opportunities for exercise, mental stimulation, and socialization, benefiting both you and your dog's overall well-being.

Outdoor Adventures

1. Exploring Nature Trails and Hiking

Embarking on nature trails or hiking adventures with your dog can be an exciting and enriching experience. Research dog-friendly trails in your area, ensure you have the necessary equipment (e.g., a leash, waste bags, water), and set off on an adventure together. Enjoy the sights, sounds, and smells of nature while providing your dog with mental and physical stimulation.

2. Beach and Water Activities

Many dogs love water, so why not take them to the beach or engage in water activities? Whether it's swimming, playing fetch in the water, or simply enjoying a leisurely stroll along the shore, these activities provide a refreshing experience for both you and your furry friend. Just ensure you choose a dog-friendly beach and prioritize water safety.

3. Agility and Obstacle Courses

Agility courses are not only a great way to challenge your dog physically but also to strengthen the bond between you. Set up an agility course in your backyard or find a local training facility where you can learn together. Jumping over hurdles, navigating tunnels, and weaving through poles are just some of the activities that can enhance your dog's coordination, agility, and problem-solving skills.

4. Outdoor Sports

Engaging in outdoor sports such as Frisbee, flyball, or fetch can provide hours of fun for you and your dog. These activities promote physical exercise, mental stimulation, and can even improve obedience skills. Find an open space, choose the appropriate equipment, and get ready for some active and enjoyable playtime.

Indoor Fun and Games

5. Interactive Puzzle Toys and Treat Dispensers

When outdoor activities are not possible, indoor play can still be engaging and entertaining. Interactive puzzle toys and treat dispensers challenge your dog's problem-solving abilities and keep them mentally stimulated. These toys require your dog to work for their treats or rewards, providing hours of fun while keeping their mind engaged.

6. Hide-and-Seek

Hide-and-seek is a classic game that can be adapted for indoor play. Start by teaching your dog to stay in one area while you hide in another part of the house. Then, call out their name or use a specific command to let them know it's time to find you. This game not only exercises their physical and mental abilities but also strengthens their bond with you.

7. Indoor Fetch or Tug-of-War

Indoor fetch can be played in a hallway or a large room with sufficient space. Choose a soft toy or a lightweight ball and play a game of fetch with your dog. Alternatively, engage in a tug-of-war session using a sturdy rope toy. These activities provide physical exercise and allow your dog to release their energy indoors.

8. Training Sessions and Tricks

Indoor playtime can also be used for training sessions and teaching your dog new tricks. Use treats and praise to motivate and reward your dog for learning and performing commands or tricks. Training not only stimulates their mind but also strengthens the bond between you and your dog.

4 | Fun And Games

Food Games

1. Hide-and-Seek Treats

Hide-and-Seek Treats is an interactive game that stimulates your dog's natural scavenging instincts. By hiding treats around the house or yard, you encourage your dog to use their nose and problem-solving skills to find the hidden rewards.

What you'll need: Your dog's favorite treats and some hiding spots.

Instructions:

1. Show your dog a treat to pique their interest.

2. While your dog watches, hide the treat in a specific location.

3. Encourage your dog to find the treat using verbal cues like "Find it!" or "Search!"

4. Celebrate their success when they discover the hidden treat by praising them and offering additional treats or a pat on the head.

2. Treat Dispensing Toys

Treat Dispensing Toys provide mental stimulation and help prevent boredom by challenging your dog to work for their treats. These toys require your dog to manipulate them in various ways to release the hidden rewards.

What you'll need: Treat-dispensing toys such as puzzle feeders or Kong toys.

Instructions:

1. Fill the treat-dispensing toy with your dog's favorite treats or kibble.

2. Show your dog how the toy works by manipulating it to release the treats.

3. Encourage your dog to interact with the toy and figure out how to extract the treats.

4. Offer verbal praise and rewards when they successfully retrieve the treats from the toy.

3. Snuffle Mat Game

The Snuffle Mat Game engages your dog's sense of smell and provides mental stimulation as they search for treats hidden within a mat filled with fabric strips.

What you'll need: A snuffle mat (a mat with fabric strips for hiding treats) or a towel.

Instructions:

1. Sprinkle your dog's treats or kibble onto the snuffle mat or towel, ensuring they are hidden within the fabric strips.

2. Encourage your dog to use their nose to search and sniff out the treats.

3. Celebrate their success as they find each hidden treat by praising them and offering additional treats or affection.

4. Muffin Tin Game

The Muffin Tin Game challenges your dog's problem-solving skills as they uncover hidden treats placed in a muffin tin.

What you'll need: A muffin tin and some tennis balls or plastic cups.

Instructions:

1. Place treats in some of the muffin tin cups.

2. Cover each cup with a tennis ball or plastic cup to create a hiding spot.

3. Encourage your dog to find the treats by sniffing and removing the covering objects.

4. Reward your dog with praise and additional treats when they successfully uncover the treats.

5. Cupcake Tin Game

The Cupcake Tin Game adds a twist to traditional treat-hunting activities by using a cupcake tin to hide treats for your dog to find.

What you'll need: A cupcake tin and some small treats.

Instructions:

1. Place a treat in each cup of the cupcake tin.

2. Cover each cup with a small ball of crumpled paper or a toy.

3. Encourage your dog to uncover the treats by removing the covers.

4. Reward your dog with praise and treats each time they reveal a tasty surprise.

6. Tug-of-War with Treat Rope

Tug-of-War with Treat Rope combines play and rewards by incorporating treats into a game of tug-of-war.

What you'll need: A sturdy rope and some small treats.

Instructions:

1. Tie small treats at intervals along the length of the rope.

2. Engage in a game of tug-of-war with your dog, allowing them to grab and enjoy the treats as they pull on the rope.

3. Use positive reinforcement by praising your dog during play and offering additional treats or rewards.

7. Find the Treats in a Box

Find the Treats in a Box is a game that challenges your dog's searching abilities as they dig through crumpled paper to find hidden treats.

What you'll need: A cardboard box, crumpled paper, and treats.

Instructions:

1. Place treats inside the cardboard box and cover them with crumpled paper.

2. Allow your dog to use their nose and paws to dig through the paper and find the hidden treats.

3. Celebrate their success by praising them and offering additional treats or affection.

8. Bobbing for Treats

Bobbing for Treats is a water-based game that adds excitement and a physical challenge as your dog tries to retrieve treats from a water-filled bucket or basin.

What you'll need: A large bucket or basin filled with water and some floating treats.

Instructions:

1. Place the floating treats in the water-filled bucket or basin.

2. Encourage your dog to use their snout or mouth to retrieve the treats from the water.

3. Monitor them closely to ensure their safety and offer positive reinforcement for their efforts.

9. Snack Stash Game

The Snack Stash Game challenges your dog to find hidden treats in various locations around your home.

What you'll need: Your dog's favorite treats and different hiding spots.

Instructions:

1. Hide treats in different locations around your home, such as under pillows, behind doors, or inside shoeboxes.

2. Encourage your dog to search for the hidden treats by using verbal cues like "Find it!" or "Search!"

3. Celebrate their success each time they discover a hidden treat by praising them and offering additional treats or affection.

10. Treat Toss and Fetch

Treat Toss and Fetch combines a game of fetch with rewarding your dog with treats when they retrieve the toy.

What you'll need: Your dog's favorite treats and a toy suitable for fetching.

Instructions:

1. Show your dog the toy and let them become interested in it.

2. Toss the toy a short distance, encouraging your dog to chase after it.

3. When your dog retrieves the toy, reward them with praise and a treat.

4. Repeat the game, gradually increasing the distance of the throws and continuing to reward your dog for their successful retrieves.

Hunting Games

11. Find the Hidden Toy

Find the Hidden Toy game engages your dog's sense of smell as they search for a hidden toy.

What you'll need: Your dog's favorite toy and some hiding spots.

Instructions:

1. Show your dog the toy to get them interested in it.

2. While your dog watches, hide the toy in a specific location.

3. Encourage your dog to find the toy using verbal cues like "Find it!" or "Search!"

4. Celebrate their success when they discover the hidden toy by praising them and engaging in a playful interaction with the toy.

12. Treasure Hunt

Treasure Hunt game challenges your dog's tracking skills by searching for hidden treats or toys.

What you'll need: Small treats or toys and various hiding spots.

Instructions:

1. Hide small treats or toys in different locations around your home or yard.

2. Encourage your dog to search for the hidden treasures by using verbal cues like "Find it!" or "Search!"

3. Celebrate their success each time they find a hidden treasure by praising them and offering additional treats or playtime with the toy.

13. Retrieve and Fetch

Retrieve and Fetch game taps into your dog's retrieving instincts by fetching and bringing back objects.

What you'll need: A toy suitable for fetching.

Instructions:

1. Show your dog the toy and let them become interested in it.

2. Toss the toy a short distance, encouraging your dog to chase after it.

3. When your dog retrieves the toy, celebrate their success and encourage them to bring it back to you.

4. Reward your dog with praise and playtime with the toy after each successful retrieve.

14. Flirt Pole

Flirt Pole game mimics prey-like movements, stimulating your dog's natural hunting instincts.

What you'll need: A flirt pole (a long pole with a rope or toy attached).

Instructions:

1. Move the flirt pole in a way that mimics the movements of prey, such as quick jerks and sudden stops.

2. Encourage your dog to chase and catch the toy attached to the flirt pole.

3. Allow your dog to "win" by capturing the toy periodically to keep them engaged and satisfied.

4. Reward your dog with praise and playtime after each successful capture.

15. Lure and Chase

Lure and Chase game imitates the movements of prey, encouraging your dog to chase and capture a lure toy.

What you'll need: A lure toy (such as a flirt pole or feather wand).

Instructions:

1. Move the lure toy in a way that mimics the movements of prey, such as quick dashes and sudden changes in direction.

2. Encourage your dog to chase and capture the lure toy.

3. Allow your dog to "win" by catching the toy periodically to keep them engaged and satisfied.

4. Reward your dog with praise and playtime after each successful capture.

16. Digging for Treasure

Digging for Treasure game allows your dog to channel their natural digging instincts to uncover hidden treats or toys.

What you'll need: A designated digging area (such as a sandbox) and treats or toys.

Instructions:

1. Bury treats or toys in the designated digging area.

2. Encourage your dog to dig and search for the buried treasures.

3. Celebrate their success when they uncover the hidden treats or toys by praising them and offering additional rewards.

17. Balloon Hunt

Balloon Hunt game engages your dog's hunting instincts by popping balloons to reveal hidden treats or toys.

What you'll need: Balloons, treats or toys, and a pin or sharp object for popping the balloons.

Instructions:

1. Insert treats or toys into the uninflated balloons.

2. Inflate the balloons and scatter them around an enclosed area.

3. Encourage your dog to chase and pop the balloons to access the hidden treats or toys.

4. Celebrate their success by praising them and offering additional rewards.

18. Feather Chase

Feather Chase game imitates the movement of prey and engages your dog's hunting instincts.

What you'll need: A feather wand or fishing pole toy with feathers attached.

Instructions:

1. Move the feather wand or fishing pole toy in a way that mimics the movements of prey, such as quick darting motions.

2. Encourage your dog to chase and capture the feathers.

3. Allow your dog to "win" by catching the feathers periodically to keep them engaged and satisfied.

4. Reward your dog with praise and playtime after each successful capture.

19. Laser Pointer

Laser Pointer game stimulates your dog's chase instinct as they try to catch the elusive light.

What you'll need: A laser pointer.

Instructions:

1. Shine the laser pointer on the ground or walls in a way that mimics the movement of prey.

2. Encourage your dog to chase and follow the light.

3. Occasionally redirect the laser to a treat or toy, allowing your dog to "capture" the reward.

4. Reward your dog with praise and playtime after each session.

20. Freeze and Find

Freeze and Find game adds a challenge to the traditional hide and seek by having your dog find you when you freeze in different positions.

What you'll need: Treats and a willingness to freeze in various positions.

Instructions:

1. Start with a simple freeze position, such as standing still with your arms crossed.

2. Ask your dog to stay or have someone hold them.

3. Freeze in the chosen position and call your dog's name or use a cue phrase like "Find me!"

4. Encourage your dog to search for you and give them hints or cues if needed.

5. Celebrate their success when they find you by praising them and offering treats as a reward.

Scent Games

21. Scent Recognition

Scent Recognition game helps your dog develop the ability to identify and differentiate various scents.

What you'll need: Different scented items (e.g., cotton balls infused with different essential oils or food extracts).

Instructions:

1. Introduce your dog to each scented item, allowing them to sniff and become familiar with the scent.

2. Present two or more scented items and ask your dog to touch or indicate the specific scent you're cueing.

3. Reward your dog with praise and treats when they correctly identify the target scent.

22. Scent Trails

Scent Trails game allows your dog to follow a specific scent trail to find hidden treats or toys.

What you'll need: Treats or toys, a long leash or rope, and a scent trail (e.g., treats crushed and scattered along a path).

Instructions:

1. Create a scent trail by scattering crushed treats along a specific path or using a scent drag (a cloth with scent on it).

2. Attach your dog to a long leash or rope.

3. Walk along the scent trail, allowing your dog to follow the scent and find the hidden treats or toys.

4. Celebrate their success when they reach the end of the trail by praising them and offering rewards.

23. Scent Discrimination

Scent Discrimination game challenges your dog to identify and locate specific scents among a variety of objects.

What you'll need: Different objects (e.g., cups, boxes, or containers) and scented items (e.g., cotton balls with different scents).

Instructions:

1. Place a scented item, such as a cotton ball infused with a specific scent, inside one of the objects.

2. Arrange the objects in a row or spread them out.

3. Encourage your dog to use their nose to find the object with the matching scent.

4. Celebrate their success when they identify the correct object by praising them and offering rewards.

24. Find It in the Grass

Find It in the Grass game challenges your dog to search for treats or toys hidden in tall grass.

What you'll need: Treats or toys and an area with tall grass (can be a backyard or a designated play area).

Instructions:

1. Show your dog the treats or toys and let them sniff and see the items.

2. Hide the treats or toys in the tall grass.

3. Release your dog and give the command "Find it!"

4. Encourage your dog to search for and retrieve the hidden treats or toys.

5. Celebrate their success when they find the items by praising them and offering rewards.

25. Scented Muffin Tin

Scented Muffin Tin game challenges your dog to find treats hidden under cups in a muffin tin.

What you'll need: A muffin tin, treats, and different scents (e.g., essential oils or food extracts).

Instructions:

1. Place a treat in each cup of the muffin tin.

2. Apply different scents to some of the treats (e.g., one scent per row).

3. Show your dog the muffin tin and let them sniff and investigate.

4. Allow your dog to search for the treats and indicate the scented ones.

5. Celebrate their success when they find the scented treats by praising them and offering rewards.

26. Scented Blanket

Scented Blanket game helps your dog associate a specific scent with a reward.

What you'll need: A blanket, treats, and a specific scent (e.g., a drop of essential oil).

Instructions:

1. Place the blanket on the ground or hold it in your hand.

2. Apply the scent to a specific area of the blanket.

3. Show your dog the blanket and let them sniff the scented area.

4. Hide treats within the folds of the blanket, including some near the scented area.

5. Encourage your dog to search for and find the treats, focusing on the scented area.

6. Celebrate their success when they locate the scented treats by praising them and offering rewards.

27. Scented Cups

Scented Cups game challenges your dog to find the cup with the specific scent.

What you'll need: Cups or containers, treats, and different scents.

Instructions:

1. Place treats under each cup and let your dog see the treats being placed.

2. Apply a different scent to the bottom of one cup.

3. Shuffle the cups around to mix up their positions.

4. Encourage your dog to indicate the cup with the specific scent by pawing or touching it.

5. Celebrate their success when they identify the correct cup by praising them and offering rewards.

28. Scented Sock Search

Scented Sock Search game challenges your dog to find scented socks hidden around the house.

What you'll need: Socks, scents (e.g., essential oils or food extracts), and treats.

Instructions:

1. Apply different scents to each sock by placing a few drops of scent on the fabric.

2. Hide the scented socks in various locations around the house.

3. Encourage your dog to search for and find the scented socks.

4. Celebrate their success when they locate a scented sock by praising them and offering treats.

29. Scented Ball Pit

The Scented Ball Pit game challenges your dog to find scented treats hidden in a pit filled with balls.

What you'll need: A small pool or container, plastic balls, scented treats, and a treat dispenser.

Instructions:

1. Fill the pool or container with plastic balls.

2. Hide scented treats among the balls.

3. Encourage your dog to search for and retrieve the scented treats.

4. Celebrate their success when they find a treat by praising them and offering additional treats.

30. Scented Agility Course

The Scented Agility Course combines agility training with scent games, challenging your dog's physical and mental abilities.

What you'll need: Agility equipment (e.g., hurdles, tunnels, weave poles), scented markers (e.g., cones with different scents), and treats.

Instructions:

1. Set up an agility course using the equipment.

2. Place scented markers at different stations throughout the course.

3. Guide your dog through the course, encouraging them to follow the scent markers and complete each obstacle.

4. Reward your dog with treats and praise at the end of each successful completion.

Agility and Balancing Games

31. Jumping Hurdles

Jumping Hurdles game challenges your dog to jump over hurdles at different heights.

What you'll need: Adjustable hurdles or makeshift obstacles, treats, and a treat dispenser.

Instructions:

1. Set up the hurdles at a low height initially.

2. Encourage your dog to jump over the hurdles one by one.

3. Gradually increase the height of the hurdles as your dog becomes more comfortable and confident.

4. Reward your dog with treats and praise after each successful jump.

32. Tunnel Dash

Tunnel Dash game involves your dog running through a tunnel.

What you'll need: A tunnel designed for dogs and treats.

Instructions:

1. Place the tunnel in an open area.

2. Encourage your dog to enter one end of the tunnel and run through to the other end.

3. Use treats to motivate your dog and guide them through the tunnel if needed.

4. Celebrate their success by praising them and offering rewards.

33. Balance Beam

Balance Beam game challenges your dog's balance and coordination skills by walking on a narrow beam.

What you'll need: A sturdy wooden beam or a commercial dog balance beam, treats, and a treat dispenser.

Instructions:

1. Place the balance beam on a non-slip surface.

2. Encourage your dog to walk on the beam, starting with a low height.

3. Guide them with treats and rewards for maintaining balance and walking along the beam.

4. Increase the difficulty by raising the height of the beam gradually.

34. Weave Poles

Weave Poles game trains your dog to navigate through a series of closely spaced poles.

What you'll need: Weave poles or a set of upright poles, treats, and a treat dispenser.

Instructions:

1. Set up the weave poles in a straight line, with a slight angle if desired.

2. Lead your dog through the poles, starting with a few widely spaced poles.

3. Gradually decrease the spacing between the poles as your dog becomes more proficient.

4. Reward your dog with treats and praise after successfully weaving through the poles.

35. Balance Disc

Balance Disc game helps improve your dog's balance and stability by standing or walking on a wobbly surface.

What you'll need: A balance disc designed for dogs, treats, and a treat dispenser.

Instructions:

1. Introduce your dog to the balance disc and allow them to sniff and investigate.

2. Encourage your dog to stand or walk on the balance disc.

3. Use treats to reward your dog for maintaining balance and stability on the disc.

4. Gradually increase the difficulty by introducing gentle movements or tilting the disc slightly.

36. A-Frame Climb

A-Frame Climb game challenges your dog to climb up and down an A-frame obstacle.

What you'll need: An A-frame obstacle or makeshift ramp, treats, and a treat dispenser.

Instructions:

1. Guide your dog to the base of the A-frame.

2. Encourage them to climb up the A-frame and reach the top.

3. Use treats and rewards to motivate and reinforce their climbing behavior.

4. Guide them down the other side of the A-frame and reward their successful descent.

37. Balancing Trick

Balancing Trick game involves teaching your dog to balance an object on their nose or head.

What you'll need: Lightweight objects that can be balanced (e.g., small plastic cones or balls), treats, and a treat dispenser.

Instructions:

1. Start by holding the object near your dog's nose and reward them for keeping their nose still.

2. Gradually place the object on their nose, rewarding them for maintaining balance.

3. Once your dog is comfortable balancing the object on their nose, introduce the cue command (e.g., "balance").

4. Reward your dog for successfully balancing the object and gradually increase the duration.

38. Hoop Jump

Hoop Jump game challenges your dog to jump through a hoop.

What you'll need: A hoop or a makeshift hoop, treats, and a treat dispenser.

Instructions:

1. Hold the hoop low to the ground and encourage your dog to walk through it.

2. Gradually raise the height of the hoop as your dog becomes comfortable.

3. Reward your dog with treats and praise after each successful jump through the hoop.

4. Increase the challenge by introducing multiple hoops or changing the angle of the hoop.

39. Balance Ball

Balance Ball game challenges your dog's balance and stability by standing or walking on a large exercise ball.

What you'll need: A large exercise ball designed for dogs, treats, and a treat dispenser.

Instructions:

1. Introduce your dog to the balance ball and allow them to investigate.

2. Encourage your dog to stand or walk on the ball, starting with a low height.

3. Use treats and rewards to reinforce their balance and stability on the ball.

4. Gradually increase the difficulty by introducing gentle movements or rolling the ball slightly.

40. Zigzag Cone Run

Zigzag Cone Run game challenges your dog to navigate through a series of cones placed in a zigzag pattern.

What you'll need: Cones, treats, and a treat dispenser.

Instructions:

1. Set up the cones in a zigzag pattern with adequate spacing between them.

2. Lead your dog through the cones, encouraging them to weave in and out.

3. Reward your dog with treats and praise after successfully navigating the zigzag pattern.

4. Increase the difficulty by decreasing the spacing between the cones or adding more cones.

Water Games

41. Splash and Retrieve

Splash and Retrieve game involves throwing a floating toy into the water for your dog to retrieve.

What you'll need: Floating toys (e.g., rubber toys, balls, or frisbees).

Instructions:

1. Stand near the water's edge and throw the floating toy into the water.

2. Encourage your dog to swim out and retrieve the toy.

3. Once your dog brings the toy back, reward them with praise and play again.

42. Water Fetch

Water Fetch game is a classic game of fetch in the water.

What you'll need: Floating toys (e.g., rubber toys, balls, or floating sticks).

Instructions:

1. Stand in shallow water and throw the toy into the water.

2. Encourage your dog to swim out and retrieve the toy.

3. When your dog brings the toy back, reward them and throw the toy again.

43. Hose Sprinkler Fun

Hose Sprinkler Fun game involves playing with a hose or sprinkler for your dog to chase and run through the water.

What you'll need: Garden hose with a spray nozzle or a sprinkler.

Instructions:

1. Set up the hose or sprinkler in an open area.

2. Turn on the water to create a gentle spray or sprinkle.

3. Encourage your dog to chase and run through the water.

4. Join in the fun by running alongside your dog or spraying water towards them.

44. Water Tug-of-War

Water Tug-of-War game is a water-based version of the classic game, using a water-soaked rope or floating tug toy.

What you'll need: Water-soaked rope or floating tug toy.

Instructions:

1. Stand in shallow water and hold one end of the rope or toy.

2. Encourage your dog to grab onto the other end and engage in a friendly tug-of-war.

3. Be mindful of your dog's strength and size to ensure a safe and enjoyable game.

45. Water Maze

Water Maze game challenges your dog to navigate through a series of floating obstacles in the water.

What you'll need: Floating objects (e.g., pool noodles, floating toys, or buoys).

Instructions:

1. Place the floating objects in the water, creating a maze-like structure.

2. Guide your dog through the maze, encouraging them to swim around or through the obstacles.

3. Reward your dog with praise and treats for successfully navigating the water maze.

46. Sprinkler Limbo

Sprinkler Limbo game combines the fun of a sprinkler with a limbo challenge for your dog to duck under the water.

What you'll need: Garden hose with a spray nozzle or a low sprinkler.

Instructions:

1. Set up the hose or sprinkler to create a low, arched stream of water.

2. Encourage your dog to walk or run under the water stream without touching it.

3. Reward your dog for successfully limbo-ing under the water and repeat the game.

47. Water Slide

Water Slide game involves creating a gentle water slide for your dog to slide into the water.

What you'll need: A pool slide or a makeshift slide with a water source.

Instructions:

1. Set up the pool slide or create a makeshift slide with a water source.

2. Encourage your dog to climb the slide and slide down into the water.

3. Reward your dog for their brave slide and repeat the game.

48. Water Race

Water Race game involves racing your dog in the water to see who can swim the fastest.

What you'll need: Open water area or a swimming pool.

Instructions:

1. Stand at one end of the water area or pool, and encourage your dog to stand at the other end.

2. Give a signal or command to start, and both you and your dog swim towards each other.

3. Celebrate and reward your dog for reaching you, and repeat the race multiple times.

49. *Water Obstacle Course*

Water Obstacle Course game involves creating a course with various water-based obstacles for your dog to navigate through.

What you'll need: Floating objects, pool noodles, hoops, and other water-safe materials.

Instructions:

1. Set up a course in the water with floating objects, pool noodles, and hoops.

2. Guide your dog through the course, encouraging them to jump over, swim under, or weave through the obstacles.

3. Reward your dog for completing each section of the course and celebrate their success.

50. *Water Polo*

Water Polo game is a canine version of the popular sport, involving passing and scoring goals with a floating ball.

What you'll need: A floating ball and two goals (could be floating objects or markers).

Instructions:

1. Place the goals at opposite ends of the water area.

2. Pass the floating ball between you and your dog, attempting to score goals by getting the ball into the opposing goal.

3. Celebrate each goal and encourage fair play by taking turns between you and your dog.

Focus Games

51. Name Recognition

Name Recognition game involves teaching your dog to respond to their name.

What you'll need: Treats and a quiet environment.

Instructions:

1. Say your dog's name in a calm and clear tone.

2. As soon as they look at you or respond, reward them with a treat and praise.

3. Repeat this exercise in different locations and gradually increase distractions.

52. Find It

Find It game encourages your dog to use their nose to locate hidden treats or toys.

What you'll need: Treats or toys and a designated hiding spot.

Instructions:

1. Show your dog a treat or toy and let them sniff it.

2. While your dog is watching, hide the treat or toy in a nearby location.

3. Say "Find it!" or a similar command and encourage your dog to search for the hidden item.

4. Reward your dog when they find the item and repeat the game with different hiding spots.

53. Follow the Finger

Follow the Finger game teaches your dog to track your finger with their eyes and maintain focus.

What you'll need: Treats and a quiet environment.

Instructions:

1. Hold a treat in one hand and extend your other hand with your finger pointing.

2. Slowly move your finger in different directions while keeping your dog's attention.

3. Reward your dog with the treat when they follow your finger with their eyes.

4. Gradually increase the difficulty by moving your finger faster or in more complex patterns.

54. Cup Game

Cup Game challenges your dog to find the treat under one of several cups.

What you'll need: Cups (3-5) and treats.

Instructions:

1. Show your dog a treat and let them see you place it under one of the cups.

2. Shuffle the cups around to mix up their positions.

3. Encourage your dog to find the cup with the treat by sniffing or pawing at it.

4. Reward your dog when they choose the correct cup and repeat the game with different arrangements.

55. Stairway Game

Stairway Game helps your dog focus on climbing or descending stairs in a controlled manner.

What you'll need: A staircase and treats.

Instructions:

1. Stand at the top or bottom of the staircase with your dog on a leash.

2. Begin to climb or descend the stairs slowly, encouraging your dog to follow you.

3. Reward your dog with a treat and praise for each step they take correctly.

4. Repeat the exercise, gradually increasing the speed and adding more steps.

56. The Statue Game

The Statue Game improves your dog's impulse control by teaching them to remain still.

What you'll need: Treats and a quiet environment.

Instructions:

1. Ask your dog to sit or stand in front of you.

2. Say "Statue" or a similar command and hold your hand up like a stop sign.

3. Count to a few seconds and reward your dog with a treat for staying still.

4. Gradually increase the duration before rewarding and introduce distractions.

57. Hide and Seek

Hide and Seek game encourages your dog to find you or another person in a designated area.

What you'll need: Treats and a hiding spot.

Instructions:

1. Ask your dog to stay or have someone hold them.

2. Find a hiding spot in the designated area and call your dog's name or use a command.

3. When your dog finds you, reward them with treats and praise.

4. Repeat the game with different hiding spots and participants.

58. Guess the Hand

Guess the Hand game challenges your dog to choose the correct hand holding a treat.

What you'll need: Treats and two closed hands.

Instructions:

1. Show your dog a treat and place it in one of your hands.

2. Close both hands, making sure your dog can't see the treat.

3. Extend your hands toward your dog and encourage them to choose the hand with the treat.

4. Reward your dog when they choose the correct hand and repeat the game multiple times.

59. Memory Game

Memory Game challenges your dog to remember the location of hidden treats or toys.

What you'll need: Treats or toys and several cups or objects to cover them.

Instructions:

1. Show your dog a treat or toy and let them sniff it.

2. While your dog is watching, place the treat or toy under one of the cups or objects.

3. Shuffle the cups or objects around to mix up their positions.

4. Encourage your dog to find the hidden treat or toy by uncovering the correct cup or object.

5. Reward your dog when they uncover the correct one and repeat the game with different arrangements.

60. Time Out

Time Out game teaches your dog self-control by rewarding them for staying calm during distractions.

What you'll need: Treats and distractions (e.g., toys, other people).

Instructions:

1. Begin with your dog on a leash and introduce a distraction, such as someone walking by or a toy being tossed.

2. When your dog remains calm and doesn't react to the distraction, reward them with a treat and praise.

3. Gradually increase the level of distractions and reward your dog for maintaining composure.

Impulse Control Games

61. Wait for the Food

This game teaches your dog to wait patiently for their food until you give them the cue to eat.

What you'll need: Your dog's food bowl and treats.

Instructions:

1. Hold your dog's food bowl and ask them to sit or wait.

2. Gradually lower the food bowl while keeping it out of your dog's reach.

3. If your dog remains calm and waits, give them a release cue (e.g., "Okay") to start eating.

4. Reward your dog with treats and praise for waiting calmly.

62. Toy Tug with Control

This game helps your dog develop impulse control during a game of tug-of-war.

What you'll need: A sturdy tug toy.

Instructions:

1. Initiate a game of tug-of-war with your dog using the tug toy.

2. Pause the game periodically and ask your dog to "Drop it" or "Leave it."

3. Reward your dog with praise and a treat when they release the toy.

4. Resume the game and repeat the process to reinforce impulse control.

63. Leave it and Take it

This game teaches your dog to leave an item on the ground until you give them permission to take it.

What you'll need: Treats and objects your dog finds tempting (e.g., toys, food).

Instructions:

1. Show your dog a tempting item in your hand.

2. Say "Leave it" in a firm but calm voice and close your hand.

3. Wait for your dog to stop showing interest in the item.

4. Open your hand and reward your dog with a treat.

5. Practice this game with different objects and gradually increase the difficulty.

64. Impulse Control with Doorways

This game helps your dog learn to wait at doorways until given permission to pass through.

What you'll need: Treats and a doorway.

Instructions:

1. Stand in front of a doorway with your dog on a leash.

2. Say "Wait" or a similar command and slowly open the door.

3. If your dog tries to pass through, gently close the door and say "Oops."

4. When your dog remains calm and waits, give them a release cue (e.g., "Okay") to pass through.

5. Reward your dog with treats and praise for waiting patiently.

65. Name Game

This game helps your dog practice impulse control by waiting until you call their name before giving attention or treats.

What you'll need: Treats.

Instructions:

1. Sit or kneel in front of your dog with treats in your hand.

2. Say your dog's name and wait for them to make eye contact or focus on you.

3. Once your dog is attentive, reward them with a treat and praise.

4. Repeat this game, gradually increasing the duration of eye contact before giving the reward.

66. It's Your Choice

This game encourages your dog to make the right choices by ignoring distractions and focusing on you.

What you'll need: Treats and distractions (e.g., toys, food).

Instructions:

1. Hold a treat in your hand and present it to your dog.

2. If your dog tries to grab the treat without permission, close your hand.

3. Wait for your dog to back away or lose interest in the treat.

4. Open your hand and reward your dog when they show self-control.

5. Repeat the game, gradually increasing the level of distractions.

67. Red Light, Green Light

This game helps your dog practice self-control by stopping when you say "Red Light" and moving when you say "Green Light."

What you'll need: Treats and a clear space to move around.

Instructions:

1. Walk with your dog on a leash and periodically stop.

2. Say "Red Light" and stop walking. Wait for your dog to also stop.

3. Give your dog a treat and say "Green Light" to resume walking.

4. Repeat the game, gradually increasing the duration of the stops.

68. Impulse Control with Food

This game teaches your dog to resist the temptation of food until you give them permission to eat.

What you'll need: Treats and your dog's food bowl.

Instructions:

1. Place your dog's food bowl on the ground.

2. Hold a treat in your hand and cover the food bowl with your other hand.

3. Say "Wait" or a similar command and wait for your dog to remain calm.

4. Give your dog a release cue (e.g., "Okay") to eat their food and reward them with a treat.

69. Drop It

This game teaches your dog to drop or release an item on command.

What you'll need: Treats and an item your dog enjoys playing with (e.g., a ball, toy).

Instructions:

1. Start a play session with your dog using the item they enjoy.

2. Say "Drop it" and show them a treat in your hand.

3. When your dog releases the item, reward them with the treat and praise.

4. Repeat the game, gradually increasing the duration of holding the item before giving the command.

70. Boundary Game

This game teaches your dog to stay within a designated area until given permission to leave.

What you'll need: Treats and a designated boundary (e.g., a mat or boundary markers).

Instructions:

1. Place your dog's bed or a mat on the floor as the designated boundary.

2. Ask your dog to go to the boundary and give the command "Stay" or "Boundary."

3. Reward your dog with treats and praise for staying within the boundary.

4. Gradually increase the duration before giving the release cue.

Mental Health and Cognitive Games

71. Shell Game

The Shell Game tests your dog's memory and scent-tracking abilities as they try to locate the hidden treat under one of three cups.

What you'll need: Three identical cups or bowls and a treat.

Instructions:

1. Show your dog the treat and then place it under one of the cups.

2. Shuffle the cups around to confuse your dog.

3. Encourage your dog to use their nose or paw to indicate which cup they believe the treat is hidden under.

4. Reward your dog when they choose the correct cup by praising them and offering the treat as a reward.

72. Which Hand

This game challenges your dog's ability to use their sense of smell to identify which hand contains the hidden treat.

What you'll need: Treats and your hands.

Instructions:

1. Show your dog the treat and let them sniff it.

2. Close your hands, one with the treat and one empty.

3. Offer both closed hands to your dog, palms facing up.

4. Encourage your dog to choose the correct hand by sniffing and pawing at it.

5. Celebrate and reward your dog when they choose the correct hand.

73. Staircase Challenge

This game challenges your dog's cognitive skills by teaching them to navigate stairs using commands.

What you'll need: A staircase.

Instructions:

1. Start with a few steps on the staircase and ask your dog to wait at the bottom.

2. Climb up the stairs and call your dog to "Come" or use a specific command.

3. Encourage your dog to climb the stairs and reward them with treats and praise.

4. Gradually increase the number of stairs your dog needs to climb.

74. Shape Sorter

This game challenges your dog's problem-solving abilities by sorting objects based on shape.

What you'll need: A shape sorter toy or several objects of different shapes.

Instructions:

1. Introduce your dog to the shape sorter toy or the objects with different shapes.

2. Show your dog how to place the objects into the corresponding holes or containers based on shape.

3. Encourage your dog to explore and figure out how to fit the objects into the right places.

4. Celebrate and reward your dog when they successfully complete the task.

75. Mimic Me

This game tests your dog's ability to imitate your actions.

What you'll need: Treats and a space for movement.

Instructions:

1. Perform a simple action, such as clapping your hands or tapping your foot.

2. Give your dog a cue, such as "Do it" or "Copy me."

3. Encourage your dog to imitate your action by performing a similar behavior.

4. Reward your dog when they successfully mimic your action.

5. Repeat with different actions and gradually increase the complexity.

76. Toy Puzzle Box

A toy puzzle box challenges your dog's problem-solving skills by requiring them to figure out how to open compartments or drawers to access hidden treats or toys.

What you'll need: A toy puzzle box or a container with compartments, treats or toys.

Instructions:

1. Introduce your dog to the toy puzzle box and let them explore it.

2. Place treats or toys in the compartments or drawers of the puzzle box.

3. Encourage your dog to interact with the puzzle box and figure out how to open each compartment to retrieve the rewards.

4. Provide guidance or hints if necessary to help your dog solve the puzzle.

5. Celebrate when your dog successfully opens the compartments and gets the treats or toys.

77. The "Clean Up" Game

The "Clean Up" game teaches your dog to tidy up their toys and promotes obedience and cooperation.

What you'll need: Your dog's toys and a designated container for toy storage.

Instructions:

1. Teach your dog the command "Clean up" or any similar cue associated with the task.

2. Encourage your dog to pick up a toy and bring it to the designated container.

3. Reward and praise your dog each time they successfully place a toy in the container.

4. Gradually increase the difficulty by adding more toys and reinforcing the command.

5. Celebrate and reward your dog when they tidy up their toys.

78. Doggie Soccer

Doggie Soccer combines physical exercise and mental stimulation as your dog learns to push a ball towards a goal.

What you'll need: A large, soft ball and a goal (can be makeshift or purchased).

Instructions:

1. Introduce the ball to your dog and let them interact with it.

2. Encourage your dog to use their nose or paws to push the ball towards the goal.

3. Guide your dog's actions and reward them when they successfully make contact with the ball.

4. Gradually increase the distance between your dog and the goal to make it more challenging.

5. Celebrate and reward your dog when they score a goal.

79. Target Stick

Target Stick game involves teaching your dog to touch a target stick with their nose or paw.

What you'll need: A target stick (e.g., a stick with a ball or a clicker), treats, and a treat dispenser.

Instructions:

1. Present the target stick to your dog and reward them for touching it with their nose or paw.

2. Gradually move the target stick to different positions and reward your dog for targeting it.

3. Introduce the cue command (e.g., "touch") and reward your dog for targeting on command.

4. Increase the difficulty by placing the target stick in higher or more challenging positions.

80. Tunnel Crawl

Tunnel Crawl game challenges your dog to crawl through a narrow tunnel.

What you'll need: A low and narrow tunnel designed for dogs, treats, and a treat dispenser.

Instructions:

1. Guide your dog to the entrance of the tunnel and encourage them to crawl through.

2. Use treats and rewards to motivate and guide them through the tunnel.

3. Celebrate their success at the other end of the tunnel by praising them and offering treats.

4. Gradually increase the length or add curves to the tunnel for added challenge.

Indoor Games - Fun Inside the House

81. Bottle Bowling

Bottle Bowling is a game that allows your dog to use their nose or paws to knock down plastic bottles.

What you'll need: Empty plastic bottles and treats.

Instructions:

1. Set up empty plastic bottles in a triangular formation, similar to a bowling alley.

2. Place treats or kibble inside some of the bottles.

3. Encourage your dog to knock down the bottles to find the hidden treats.

4. Reward your dog with treats for successful knockdowns.

82. Simon Says

Simon Says is a game that tests your dog's obedience and listening skills.

What you'll need: Treats.

Instructions:

1. Give your dog a command, such as "Sit" or "Lie Down."

2. If your dog performs the command correctly, reward them with a treat.

3. If you say "Simon Says" before the command, your dog should obey and receive a treat.

4. If you give a command without saying "Simon Says" and your dog performs it, they should not receive a treat.

83. Sock Tug

Sock Tug is a gentle game that allows your dog to engage in interactive play with a sock.

What you'll need: A clean sock.

Instructions:

1. Hold one end of the sock while your dog grabs the other end with their mouth.

2. Gently tug back and forth, allowing your dog to pull on the sock.

3. Maintain a relaxed grip and avoid excessive pulling to prevent the sock from tearing.

4. Reward your dog with praise and playtime for participating.

84. Obstacle Course

Creating an obstacle course in your house provides physical exercise and mental stimulation for your dog.

What you'll need: Household items like pillows, chairs, and tunnels.

Instructions:

1. Arrange pillows to create hurdles for your dog to jump over.

2. Place chairs or tables in a zigzag pattern to create weaving poles.

3. Use blankets or tunnels for your dog to crawl through.

4. Guide your dog through the obstacle course, using treats and praise as motivation.

85. Musical Mats

Musical Mats is a dog-friendly version of musical chairs that tests your dog's listening and obedience skills.

What you'll need: Mats or towels and treats.

Instructions:

1. Place mats or towels in a circle on the floor, one fewer than the number of participants.

2. Play music and have your dog walk or run around the circle of mats.

3. When the music stops, call out a command like "Sit" or "Down."

4. Your dog should quickly obey the command and sit on a mat.

5. Remove one mat each round until only one mat is left, and the last dog sitting on the mat wins a treat.

86. Doggie Basketball

Doggie Basketball is a game that combines physical activity with mental stimulation as your dog learns to put a ball into a basket.

What you'll need: A small ball and a basket or hoop.

Instructions:

1. Place the basket or hoop at a suitable height for your dog.

2. Show your dog the ball and encourage them to grab it with their mouth.

3. Guide your dog to bring the ball to the basket and drop it inside.

4. Once your dog effectively constructs a basket, you should praise them and give them treats as an incentive.

87. Newspaper Search

The Newspaper Search game engages your dog's sense of smell as they search for hidden treats among crumpled newspapers.

What you'll need: Newspapers and treats.

Instructions:

1. Crumple several sheets of newspaper into balls.

2. Hide treats within the crumpled newspapers.

3. Scatter the newspaper balls around the room.

4. Encourage your dog to sniff out and find the treats hidden within the newspapers.

88. Treat Maze

The Treat Maze game challenges your dog's problem-solving abilities as they navigate through a maze to find hidden treats.

What you'll need: Cardboard, scissors, treats, and tape.

Instructions:

1. Cut a piece of cardboard into a maze-like structure with dead ends and multiple pathways.

2. Place treats at different points within the maze.

3. Show your dog a treat and let them see you place it at the start of the maze.

4. Encourage your dog to navigate through the maze to find the treats.

5. Guide them with verbal cues or gestures if needed and reward them when they locate the treats.

89. Balloon Volleyball

Balloon Volleyball is a game that promotes physical activity and coordination as your dog tries to keep a balloon from touching the ground.

What you'll need: A balloon and an open space in your house.

Instructions:

1. Blow up a balloon and lightly toss it in the air.

2. Encourage your dog to use their paws or nose to keep the balloon from touching the ground.

3. Engage in a playful back-and-forth volley with your dog.

4. Celebrate and reward your dog when they successfully keep the balloon in the air.

90. Treat Limbo

Treat Limbo is a game that tests your dog's flexibility and coordination as they navigate under a "limbo stick" to retrieve treats.

What you'll need: A broomstick or a similar object and treats.

Instructions:

1. Hold the broomstick horizontally at a low height, allowing your dog to easily go under it.

2. Encourage your dog to go under the stick by luring them with a treat.

3. Gradually lower the stick to make it more challenging for your dog to pass under.

4. Reward your dog with treats when they successfully navigate under the stick.

5. Adjust the height of the stick based on your dog's abilities.

Teaching To Play With Kids

91. Ball Pit Fun

Ball pits are a playful and interactive way for your child and your dog to enjoy sensory stimulation and gentle physical activity.

What you'll need: A small inflatable pool or a large container filled with soft, child-safe balls.

Instructions:

1. Create a safe and contained area using the inflatable pool or a designated space.

2. Fill the pool or container with soft balls.

3. Encourage your child and your dog to explore and play within the ball pit.

4. Use toys or treats to engage your dog, encouraging them to interact with the balls.

5. Supervise the playtime to ensure safety and prevent swallowing of the balls.

92. Bubble Fun

Playing with bubbles is an entertaining activity that can capture your dog's attention and engage your child in interactive play.

What you'll need: Bubble solution and bubble wand.

Instructions:

1. Create a safe and open space for bubble play.

2. Have your child blow bubbles using the bubble wand.

3. Encourage your dog to chase and pop the bubbles.

4. Celebrate and reward your dog's interaction with the bubbles.

5. Ensure that the bubble solution is non-toxic and safe for your dog to avoid ingestion.

93. Puppet Show

Puppet Show is an imaginative game where your child can create a puppet show and involve your dog as an audience member.

What you'll need: Puppets or stuffed animals.

Instructions:

1. Have your child set up a small puppet show area using a table or cardboard box.

2. Encourage your child to put on a puppet show, telling a story or acting out a scene.

3. Invite your dog to sit or lie down as the audience member, watching the show.

4. Praise your dog for their calm behavior and engage them with treats or gentle petting during breaks.

5. Enjoy the creative performance together.

94. Paw Painting

Paw Painting is a creative activity where your child and dog can collaborate to create unique artwork using their paws.

What you'll need: Non-toxic and washable paint, large paper or canvas, water, and towels.

Instructions:

1. Prepare the painting area by laying down the large paper or canvas.

2. Dip your dog's paw in a small amount of non-toxic paint.

3. Guide your dog's paw onto the paper or canvas to create paw prints.

4. Have your child use their hands or brushes to add additional artistic elements.

5. Repeat the process with different colors and patterns, creating a collaborative masterpiece.

95. Snack Toss

Snack Toss is a game that improves your dog's catching skills and hand-eye coordination for your child.

What you'll need: Dog-friendly treats or small toys.

Instructions:

1. Have your child stand a short distance away from your dog, holding a treat or toy.

2. Encourage your child to toss the treat or toy gently towards your dog.

3. Your dog should catch the treat or retrieve the toy in their mouth.

4. Praise and reward your dog for successfully catching or retrieving the item.

5. Gradually increase the distance and challenge your dog's catching abilities.

96. Doggie Dress-Up

Doggie Dress-Up is a game that involves your child dressing up your dog in fun costumes or accessories.

What you'll need: Dog-friendly costumes or accessories.

Instructions:

1. Gather a selection of dog-friendly costumes or accessories.

2. Have your child choose a costume or accessory and help them dress up your dog.

3. Take pictures and make it a fun photo session.

4. Ensure your dog is comfortable and not stressed by the outfits.

5. Enjoy the bonding experience and share laughs as you dress up your dog together.

97. Musical Sit

Musical Sit is a variation of the classic musical chairs game that involves your dog and your kid.

What you'll need: Chairs or mats, and some upbeat music.

Instructions:

1. Arrange chairs or mats in a circle, facing outward.

2. Start playing upbeat music and have your child walk or dance around the chairs.

3. When the music stops, your child must find a chair and sit down, and your dog must also sit beside them.

4. Remove one chair each round, and continue playing until there's only one chair left.

5. The last round can be a race between your child and your dog to see who can sit down first.

98. Stuffed Animal Tag

Use a stuffed animal as the "tagger" in a game of tag between your child and dog.

What you'll need: A stuffed animal.

Instructions:

1. Select a stuffed animal to be the "tagger" and have your child hold it.

2. Encourage your child to tag your dog with the stuffed animal, initiating a game of chase.

3. Once your dog is tagged, they can then become the "tagger" and chase your child.
4. Ensure that everyone plays gently and safely, avoiding rough movements or excessive chasing.

99. Agility Tunnel Races

Set up an agility tunnel and have your child and dog race through it, promoting agility and speed.

What you'll need: An agility tunnel.

Instructions:

1. Set up the agility tunnel in a clear space inside your home.

2. Have your child and dog stand on opposite ends of the tunnel.

3. On your signal, encourage both your child and dog to race through the tunnel as fast as they can. 4. Celebrate when they reach the other end of the tunnel.

4. Repeat the race, trying to beat their previous times and adding fun challenges along the way.

100. Toy Fetch Relay

Set up a relay race where your child and dog take turns fetching toys and bringing them back to a designated spot.

What you'll need: Dog toys and a designated spot for returning the toys.

Instructions:

1. Have your child and dog stand at opposite ends of the room.

2. Give your child a toy and instruct them to throw it to your dog.

3. Encourage your dog to fetch the toy and bring it back to the designated spot.

4. Celebrate when they successfully complete the relay, and then switch roles.

5. Time each relay race to add an element of friendly competition.

In this book, we have explored various aspects of dog care and training that can contribute to making your dog happy and peaceful. We have discussed the importance of understanding your dog's needs, providing proper care, and implementing effective training techniques. By following the guidelines presented in this book, you can create a nurturing and loving environment for your furry friend.

Throughout the chapters, we have learned about the essential commands that your dog should learn for obedience. These commands not only establish control but also foster a strong bond between you and your dog. By incorporating positive reinforcement and consistency in your training sessions, you can effectively teach these commands and promote obedience in your dog.

We have also emphasized the significance of creating a constructive educational environment for your dog. By providing mental stimulation through interactive play, puzzle toys, and training exercises, you can enhance their cognitive development and prevent boredom. Engaging in playtime with your dog is not only enjoyable but also crucial for their overall well-being.

Moreover, we have discussed the importance of encouragement through rewards rather than punishment. Positive reinforcement techniques, such as treats, praise, and affection, can motivate your dog to learn and obey commands. Avoiding punishment-based methods not only prevents unnecessary stress and fear in your dog but also helps build a trusting and loving relationship between you and your furry companion.

Additionally, we have explored different types of games and activities that can enhance the fun factor for human-dog teams. From outdoor activities like fetch, agility training, and water games to indoor games such as hide-and-seek and puzzle-solving, these activities provide exercise, mental stimulation, and socialization opportunities for both you and your dog. By engaging in these activities, you can strengthen the bond with your dog and create lasting memories.

Let's summarize the key things to do and things to avoid to ensure the well-being of your dog.

Things to Do:

1. Understand Your Dog's Needs: Take the time to understand your dog's breed characteristics, temperament, and individual preferences. This knowledge will help you provide appropriate care, exercise, and mental stimulation tailored to their specific needs.

2. Provide Proper Nutrition: Provide your dog with a diet that is well-balanced and covers all of their nutritional needs. Your dog's age, size, and current state of health should all be factors considered by your veterinary practitioner when selecting the most appropriate diet for your pet.

3. Regular Exercise: Engage your dog in regular physical exercise to keep them fit and mentally stimulated. Daily walks, playtime, and activities such as agility training or fetch are great ways to ensure they get the exercise they need.

4. Mental Stimulation: Engage your dog's mind with mental exercises such as training sessions, puzzle toys, and scent work. These activities help prevent boredom and provide mental challenges that keep your dog happy and content.

5. Positive Reinforcement: Treats, praise, and compassion are all examples of positive reinforcement tactics that can be used to reward and promote behaviors that are preferred. This approach builds trust, strengthens the bond between you and your dog, and enhances their learning experience.

6. Establish Clear Rules and Boundaries: Consistency is key in establishing rules and boundaries for your dog. Teach them what behaviors are acceptable and reinforce these guidelines consistently. This helps them understand their place in the family and promotes good behavior.

Things to Avoid:

1. Harsh Punishment: Avoid using harsh punishment methods such as yelling, physical force, or aversive training tools. These methods can create fear and anxiety in your dog, damaging the bond between you and undermining their overall well-being.

2. Neglecting Veterinary Care: Regular veterinary check-ups are essential to monitor your dog's health, prevent illnesses, and address any concerns promptly. Neglecting veterinary care can lead to undetected health issues and unnecessary suffering for your dog.

3. Overfeeding and Unhealthy Treats: Be mindful of your dog's portion sizes and avoid overfeeding, as obesity can lead to various health problems. Additionally, choose healthy treats and avoid feeding them foods that are toxic or harmful to dogs.

4. Ignoring Exercise and Mental Stimulation: Dogs require both physical and mental exercise. Neglecting their exercise needs can lead to behavioral issues and excess energy. Make sure to provide opportunities for play, exercise, and mental stimulation daily.

5. Lack of Socialization: Socialization is crucial for dogs to develop proper behavior around people, other animals, and various environments. Avoid isolating your dog and provide opportunities for positive social interactions from an early age.

"By following the guidelines presented in this book, you can make your dog very happy and peaceful. By establishing a strong bond, providing proper care, and implementing effective training techniques, you can create a nurturing and loving environment for your furry friend. Remember to be patient, consistent, and understanding of your dog's individual needs. Your dedication and love will be rewarded with a lifelong companionship filled with joy and harmony. May you and your dog embark on a journey of happiness and contentment together".

With Love, Olivia.

Frame the QR Code with your smartphone and access the page of the Free Bonus Book
Homemade Healthy Dog Food Guide and Cookbook

I dedicate this book to my beloved 15-year-old dog, Birillo.
Each day I spend with him is truly incredible, as his presence fills my life
with immense joy and love, making every moment unique and special.

Made in the USA
Las Vegas, NV
07 October 2023

78704822R00070